Data Science $

Get Your Dream Job in Data

Jay Samson, MSc

Table Of Contents

Discover Your Path in Data

Data Analyst, Data Scientist, Data Engineer, Research Scientist, Business Operations & Strategy Analyst, Ops Analyst, Business Analyst. The data world has all of the above and many, many more roles. It doesn't matter if you're a college dropout or a PhD in computer science- with all of the options available, it can be incredibly difficult to understand what role you actually want.

This section has one intention: give you a comprehensive understanding of what role is right for you and what role you actually want. No matter how good you are, the interview process is an intense grind if you want to get something good, and without a true focus getting a great job may be impossible.

Kevin's Story

He felt ready. Kevin was brimming with confidence- he just finished a 3-month data course on Coursera in only 2 months. He struggled at times, but worked his tail off to learn the material and finish way ahead of schedule. All the early mornings, long nights, and full weekends of studying and grinding were finally about to pay off in the form of a fantastic new job in the tech industry. He'd been working as a marketing associate at a small financial services company and was told, "Just focus on your job" when he asked about transitioning into an analyst role at the company. "They didn't think I could do it, but here I am," he thought. He was ready to reap the rewards of his hard work.

He started by taking a few hours to create a spreadsheet with potential jobs he'd apply for. He began his search on LinkedIn, and was impressed by how many role openings there were (and a little overwhelmed). He started adding them to the list: first lots of small companies, then adding some big fish like Google and Amazon. And why not? Sure, he didn't go to Stanford or Harvard, but he took the initiative and learned things on his own. Maybe that would be even better than going to a blue-chip college. Despite feeling a bit overwhelmed at first, Kevin got excited as he added more jobs to his spreadsheet- soon collecting over 30 roles that looked awesome: data science, data analytics, machine learning, even a few with "Engineer" in the title that looked really cool. He had so many skills that he felt is was just a matter of finding the right company and compensation, and he'd blow it out of the water.

Kevin read that he should apply to jobs Monday morning, so the application will be at the top of the recruiter's inbox. He set aside 30 minutes to polish his resume, then another 20 minutes to make sure he had the perfect mission statement at the top. He proofread the entire document word-for-word and looked loving at the final PDF, thinking, "I'm really doing it." Then, he dove right in- going through all the links, applying and even writing cover letters when possible to give it a special touch. After a few hours he double-checked the spreadsheet to make sure he'd applied to them all. The only thing left to do was wait.

So he waited. And waited. Nothing the first day. "No big deal," he thought, "It'd be crazy if they responded within a day." He focused on his day job for the rest of the day, and then went out to get beers with a few friends after work. When they asked him about the job hunt, he excitedly told them, "I'm pretty close. I'll probably be somewhere great within a month." The next day went by- nothing. "No big deal. Recruiters are super busy anyway." He took some time to review his notes and look up interview questions from some of his top companies.

Wednesday went by. He received two rejections that looked like automated responses. Attempting to rationalize, he thought, "Maybe those roles are already filled". He frantically checked his resume to see if he misspelled his email or something. He didn't. "It's fine. They get so many applicants, so it probably just takes some time," he thought.

Thursday: no response.

Friday: no response. He met up with some of the same friends he saw earlier in the week. "Hey Kevin, any interview lined up next week?" , they asked. "Um, no, not yet. Recruiters stay pretty busy so I don't have anything on the books yet, but I'm sure it will be soon." The weekend came and went without any updates. He figured that he wouldn't get any responses on Saturday or Sunday, but he did double-check his spam folder to be sure. Nothing in there. "Weird", he thought. Staying optimistic, he spent some time researching recruiter interview questions and even writing out his responses. He wanted to make sure he was 100% prepared for the calls he was sure he'd have the following week.

Monday: no response. Now, Kevin was getting stressed, and it showed. He had to deliver a report to his boss by end of day Monday, which he did, but his boss found a few simple math errors. This made him even more stressed, and the stress was starting to turn into frustration. Kevin clenched his teeth, "I do this report every month- how did I screw this up? How am I going to work in data if I can't even do this simple stuff right?"

The rest of the week dragged on as Kevin agonized over his inbox. Opening, refreshing, opening, refreshing. Nothing. One day he got a rejection letter, but just like before it was an automated response. He wondered if maybe something was wrong with the way his resume was formatted, or if recruiters weren't noticing the Coursera credential at the bottom, so he decided to reply to one of the rejection letters and politely ask if there was any feedback. This gave him a small boost of confidence because he figured he would just implement their ideas and be good to go. Unfortunately he discovered that wouldn't be possible: "Shoot, these are no-reply emails. I can't even ask a question."

Another week went by, leaving Kevin feeling dejected. Over 30 applications and not a single interview, not even a recruiter call. Knowing that persistence is key, he decided to spend the weekend collecting application links, and as he added roles he felt the excitement again. There were so many different roles at awesome companies that he felt he was bound to get something amazing. 20 links later he shut the laptop and decided to get some sleep- tomorrow he was going to hit the pavement and send out those applications.

He woke up early and got to work. First, he combed through his resume, examining every letter of every word of every line. It was immaculate. After a few adjustments to make his mission statement even more powerful, he gave the resume one more read-through and commenced the application process. He sped through the task, only doing cover letters for the biggest companies this time. He finished up in about an hour and started getting ready for his day job. "I've got it this time", he thought.

Monday went by. No response. Tuesday was the same. Around 10:30am on Wednesday a buzzing notification from his phone made him nearly jump out of his seat.

"Finally!" he thought as he read the email: "*We'd like to schedule you for a phone call to discuss the Sales Ops role.*" This wasn't Google or anything, but it was an interesting-looking marketing technology company. He could use both his analytical skills and his marketing expertise (and maybe he'd get paid even more for having both). Kevin quickly emailed the recruiter with his availability and they scheduled the call.

He prepared. He wrote down all the questions he thought he might be asked, his answers, and even practiced saying them out loud. Kevin is no slouch. On the day of the interview he felt confident enough to climb a mountain or run through a wall.

The call began and they exchanged pleasantries quickly before getting down to business: "*Tell me about yourself*"

No problem- Kevin anticipated this question and gave a fantastic answer about his passion for analytics and how he spent most of his free time studying and learning the ropes. He could tell the recruiter was impressed.

"*What's your understanding of the Sales Ops role?*"

He wasn't planning on being asked this, but he took a moment to think and re-worded what he remembered from the job posting. Something about doing data deep dives, finding insights, and driving the strategy of the business. Not a perfect answer, but he felt it was OK. Besides, he had technical skills and let the recruiter know he's always open to learning more. The recruiter's response was a little less enthusiastic, but not bad or anything.

"*What's your experience working with sales teams?*"

"Not much" he replied, trying to make a joke. The recruiter didn't laugh, so he started talking again about his passion for data and how he's always open to learning more. Again he received a lukewarm response, but this time he just shrugged it off. "She's probably just tired. Recruiting is a very busy job," he thought.

"*What kind of work interests you?*"

Finally, one of the questions from his list. Kevin jumped right on it and started talking about how he thinks machine learning is so fascinating, and how he's spent a lot of time doing it and even did some small classification projects on his own. He even mentioned a few of his favorite models (Random Forest, Logistic

Regression) and talked about why he likes decision trees but is always looking out for overfitting. "Awesome answer!" he thought to himself once he finished.

Silence on the line. "...OK. That sounds really cool.", the recruiter said, again not sounding very excited. Kevin reminded himself that she was probably just having a long day or doesn't want to show too much emotion on these calls.

At that point the recruiter wrapped up the interview and they said their goodbyes. Kevin made sure to thank her, and when he asked about next steps she simply said, "We'll email you and let you know". This was good enough for him. He met up with some friends that night and told them all about it.

"I have a good feeling about this one." he told them. In the moment he knew that he didn't have perfect answers, but that's to be expected. Nobody gives perfect answers, right? He had a little bit of nagging worry, but not much. Kevin knew he had to just focus on the next interview, which he figured would be with the hiring manager and would probably be more challenging.

The next morning his phone buzzed again, and Kevin opened his inbox excitedly.

"Thank you for your application to ....", **the subject line read.

He quickly opened the email to read the rest:

"Thank you for applying to the Sales Operations Analyst role. We've had the privilege of talking to many great applicants, and at this time we're going to proceed with a candidate who's a stronger fit for the role."

Stunned, Kevin sat staring at the message. "Wow, really?", he thought. Kevin figured there would be some rejection, but you never quite feel it until it actually happens to you. "Oh well," he sighed, thinking about how his friends were going to ask for a status update. He wasn't looking forward to that conversation.

The rest of the week went by without any responses (except a few rejection emails). The next week came and went in a similar fashion. That weekend he sat in his room and looked down at his progress tracker. One month, 50 applications, 1 interview. Lots of rejections. "What the heck is going on?", Kevin thought to himself.

He decided to "get right back on the horse" and start applying to more jobs.

What was Kevin's problem? Was his resume bad? Was he getting rejected because he didn't go to Stanford? Did people look down on marketers? No, no, no, and no.

So what was it? Could it be that Kevin was getting rejected because he was just blasting out applications to whatever jobs looked "cool", rather than job that actually fit his skill set, experience, and interest? Let's dissect this idea.

Discover Your Path

In order to successfully make your next career move, you need to get clear on exactly what types of roles you're pursuing. You can still course-correct later and explore other options, but you need to have a specific outcome in mind if you want to actually get somewhere. Kevin didn't know what he actually wanted. He loved working with data and had the right skills, but he couldn't tell a Business Analyst from a Data Scientist from a Machine Learning Engineer.

Let's try a short exercise: Here are two actual answers people looking to begin a career in data gave to the same question: "What kind of role are you looking for?"

Person A: "I want to be a Data Scientist with a focus on analytics and the ability to apply fundamental statistical knowledge. My ideal role is one where I can flex my analytical chops and work cross-functionally to influence strategic business decisions"

Person B: "I want to work in data, and I'm really interested in doing data analysis in Python"

Which person do you think has a better chance of landing a job in data? By now, the answer should be obvious- Person A is going to understand which roles to go after and will have much more success interviewing with recruiters and hiring managers. Person B is going to struggle and may never get a job in data, let alone their ideal role.

So what does this mean for you? You probably have a basic idea of what data work interests you most, and this section is going to help you get incredibly clear on your vision and outline your specific, actionable outcome. With your outcome top-of-mind you'll increase your efficiency, need less study time, be able to speak to interviewers clearly and confidently, and most importantly- you'll dramatically increase your chance of landing your ideal role in data. Go through this section carefully and find your ideal path in data.

Let's get down to the nitty-gritty. There are a few things to think about when you're looking to start your career in data and need to choose the right path. Some examples:

How much coding do you know? How much do you want to learn?

Do you like probability and statistics? Are you willing to hit the books hard to get your stats knowledge up to par?

What's your background? Is this your first technical role, or have you had other technical roles? Be honest here ("Marketing" is not a technical role). Remember that you can still succeed if you don't have technical roles on your resume.

Are you more of a strategy person who wants to work with non-technical audiences to drive business outcomes, or are you a "behind-the-scenes" expert who keeps everything running smoothly?

We'll take a full assessment at soon, but for now let these ideas marinate. It's important to know that to start out, you won't be able to do everything, and we also have to balance what is reasonable for you at this stage in your career. For example, Machine Learning is an incredibly interesting part of the data world, but if you've only got a year of experience in a non-technical role and don't know any coding languages, it will be extremely difficult to get an ML role.

Know this: if you're attempting to get your first role in data, just getting in is more important than getting your exact, ideal role. Once you have your foot in the door, you'll be able to hustle, prove yourself, learn from more senior people, and transition into bigger and better. You can get any role you want with the right strategy and work ethic- it just may take some time to get experience and build up your skills in a business setting.

Let's get started.

Data Path Assessment

For each question, circle or write down the letter in parentheses that corresponds to your preference. There may be questions where you like both choices- just go with your gut on which one you'd like more.

I prefer:

1. Setting up systems & processes (E) | Coming up with new ideas (A)

2. Database storage and technology (E) | Running experiments on user features (S)

3. Giving presentations to leaders in the company (A) | Using probability & statistics (S)

4. Working with non-technical people (A) | Working mostly with very technical people, such as software engineers (E)

5. Machine Learning (S) | Digging into problems and finding solutions (A)

6. Coding 100% of the time (E) | A mix of coding and non-coding (experiment analysis, communicating insights, etc) (S)

7. Running experiments (S) | Creating software infrastructure (E)

8. Supporting Non-Technical Teams (A) | Supporting Technical Teams (E)

9. Using Python (S) | Using a business intelligence tool such as Tableau (A)

10. Testing a Hypothesis (S) | Building a Data Pipeline (E)

11. Creating a data visualization (A) | Creating a new metric (S)

12. Maintaining a data warehouse (E) | Writing SQL (A)

Now, add up the number of times you circled A, S, and E. The letter with the highest score is the path that your preference align with the most:

A - Data Analyst

S - Data Scientist

E - Data Engineer

Let's get clear on a few things. First of all, all three career paths touch on all the topics mentioned above. Data Scientists use SQL, Data Analysts can be involved in running experiments, so on and so forth. This quiz is meant to give you a sense of what sort of roles you should look into as you're starting your job search.

Speaking of the job search, another important thing to mention is that data roles are highly depending on a given company's naming convention. Some companies have their Data Scientists work on Engineering problems. Some companies have Data Analysts work with lots of probability and statistics (typical Data Scientist skills). Some companies don't even have a, "Data Analyst" role, and instead call this group of employees Data Scientists.

Sound confusing? It certainly can be. All we want to do right now is to understand which way you're leaning, and then we'll dig into specific roles to figure out what roles specifically will be best for your interests and abilities. Let's begin the deep dive- here are the three buckets in more detail:

Analytics

Roles: Analyst, Business Analyst, Operations Analyst, Data Analyst, Data Scientist (Analytics Focus)

An analyst's main job is to have an in-depth understanding of the company's data stores, analyze that data, and look for patterns that can be assembled into insights. Analysts typically communicate insights and recommendations to company leaders in order to drive strategy. Some questions analysts might answer:

Where should we invest in acquiring more customers?

How often do our customers cancel, and what factors drive those cancellations?

What's our go-to-market strategy for this new product?

There is an entire world of interesting work for an analyst to do at a company, particularly those in the technology space. Within the Analyst bucket there are many different roles with different responsibilities. That said, the core is the same: understand the data and use it to help drive the company forward.

Here are some of the roles in more detail:

Business Analyst: Business Analysts work closely with decision-makers to understand what the business needs and leverage data to help make decisions. For example, a business analyst may answer the question, "How do we cut waste and help our internal dashboarding tools work more efficiently?"

Operations Analyst: An Operations Analyst might do similar work as a Business Analyst. Someone in this role might be tasked with providing monthly reporting on various business processes and surfacing the most valuable insights to internal stakeholders.

Sales Operations Analyst: Sales Ops Analysts are almost always a role that supports the sales teams within a company. Some typical things this analyst may handle include pulling and packaging sales metrics, diagnosing the sales pipeline, and improving the team's productivity. If you have a background in sales, this is an excellent entry point into the world of data.

Marketing Analyst: Marketing Analysts understand marketing, but also have the technical skills to analyze the success or failure of marketing efforts. A typical day for a Marketing Analyst may include pulling lists for direct mail campaigns, analyzing email marketing campaigns, or working with a product marketing manager to test a new marketing idea. Those with a background in marketing and some technical skills often make great Marketing Analysts.

Revenue Analyst: This is an interesting role. Revenue Analysts are almost like accountants, but they get much deeper into the data and look for ways to increase revenue, as well as standard metrics reporting. This is a great move for someone who studied accounting or has worked in financial services before (and is interested in that kind of work).

Product Analyst: Product Analysts are often involved in some of the most interesting work at a company. These analysts are tasked with working on a specific product within a company (e.g. YouTube within Google), and they'll often do things like measuring usage, working with Product Managers to test new features, and evaluating product performance. If you've considered becoming a Product Manager, or just have an interest in working on the product side of a company, this may be the role for you.

Data Analyst: If this role sounds broad, it's because it is. "Data Analyst" could mean any of the above roles or be essentially a Data Scientist, depending on the company. In general the tasks of a data analyst including digging through large amounts of data, finding insights, and communicating those insights to their team and leaders in the organization. SQL is a must, and often Data Analyst role postings love to see candidates with Python experience. The Data Analyst role is a great idea for someone who wants to work in more complex data topics (hard core statistics, machine learning), but may not be quite there yet in skill set or experience.

Data Scientist (Analytics Focus): What's a "Data Scientist" title doing in here? No, it's not a typo. Lately many companies have begun to rebrand their Data Analyst roles as "Data Scientist". The reason for this is they often need candidates to be fluent in Python, and in some cases want to see a foundational knowledge of statistics. This is a great role for someone with some experience in analytical roles who's put in the extra time to learn more challenging topics.

Data Scientist

Data Scientists are the brain-center of the organization, particularly in tech companies. They can serve a very wide variety of functions, but often their basic toolkit includes great analytical knowledge, above-average ability in probability and statistics, and, depending on the role, working knowledge of machine learning.

This is one of the most difficult career buckets to dissect because there is such a wide variety of actual job functions under the "Data Scientist" title. We will go more in depth, but the best way to help yourself understand which role is right for you, and which data scientist role is right for you, is to read job postings very carefully. In some industries or company segments, job postings may be more or less arbitrary- not true with Data Science! Data Scientist role postings almost always do a great job explaining accurately what the role responsibilities will be and what the requirements are.

Here's an example of a Data Scientist role posting:

Data Scientist at ABC Corp

- Master's degree or higher in Engineering, Math, Finance, Statistics, Computer Science, or other technical field from an accredited university.

- Experience processing, filtering, and presenting large quantities (Millions to Billions of rows) of data.

- Experience articulating business questions and using quantitative techniques to arrive at a solution using available data.

- 3+ years of hands on experience with statistical analysis, causal inferences, applying various machine learning techniques (e.g. ensembling, regularization, feature engineering), predictive modeling, and data mining.

- 3+ years of experience with data querying languages (e.g. SQL), scripting languages (e.g. Python), statistical/mathematical software (e.g. R, SAS, MATLAB), and machine learning packages (e.g. scikit-learn).

- Ability to develop experimental and analytic plans for data modeling processes, use of strong baselines, ability to accurately determine cause and effect relations.

- Demonstrable track record of dealing well with ambiguity, prioritizing needs, and delivering results in a dynamic environment.

- Excellent verbal and written communication skills with the ability to effectively advocate technical solutions to research scientists, engineering teams and business audiences.

And here's another example:

Data Scientist at XYZ, Inc:

- Professional industry experience in a quantitative analysis role (4+ years preferred).

- Comfortable in SQL and some experience with a programming language, with Python or R a plus.

- Ability to communicate clearly and effectively to cross functional partners of varying technical levels.

- Ability to define relevant metrics that can guide and influence stakeholders to the appropriate and accurate insights.

- Experience or willingness to learn tools to create data pipelines.

- Building clear and easy to understand dashboards (Tableau) and presentations.

Do they look the same? Not even close. This is why it is crucial to read job postings thoroughly when you're looking for roles. If you understand the job really well, you'll maximize your chances of actually getting an interview, and when you get an interview you'll do much better.

All of that said, before you start running to apply to Data Scientist roles, make sure that these general concepts appeal to you:

- Probability & statistics
- Experimentation
- Machine learning & modeling
- Working with non-technical stakeholders

If you find all of the above interesting, the Data Scientist path may be for you. It's probably a good idea to think about which of the above appeal to you most, and which of the above areas you're strongest in. By doing this you'll be able to recognize the right role immediately and not waste time applying to roles where you wouldn't be happy and successful.

There is one specific type of role worth mentioning here, within the Data Scientist path: Research Scientist. This is an interesting role that has existed in academia for a long time, but has recently come to prominence in private industry. Often these roles look very similar to Data Scientists, but the work tends to be even more focused on experimentation and heavy-duty machine learning algorithms. Research Scientists typically have PhDs- if you are interested in Data Science and come from a very scientific background/academia, this may be the path for you.

Data Engineer

If you're not as familiar with this role, you're not alone. Ironically this job doesn't usually make it to the "Sexiest Jobs of the 21st Century" list often, but Data Science and Analytics wouldn't even be possible without Data Engineers. These people often have a background in software engineering and are responsible for building and maintaining data pipelines and data stores.

If you've ever run a SQL query, a Data Engineer (or team of them) built that database. Doing anything with data would be impossible without a reliable infrastructure to extract, clean, store, and eventually retrieve crucial data. When a user hits the "Like" button, how does that click get counted? Ask a Data Engineer.

A few notes on this role: you'll likely have to have experience in serious coding and software engineering in order to move into one of these roles, and it will be hard to do if you're purely self-taught.

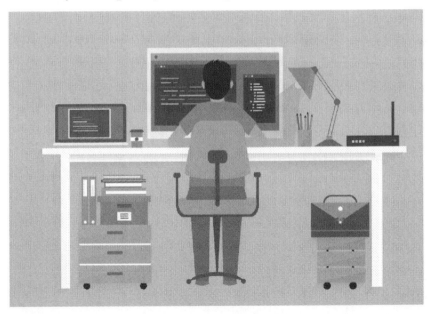

One path that many people take is to find a role that is more entry level (usually some sort of analyst), and then work their way into their ultimate, ideal role (data engineer or data scientist). This is a good idea for people who don't have a degree in a technical field or don't want to take on lots of additional education. This may actually benefit you in the long run since you'll be able to develop a very strong analytical foundation and then branch out into more challenging topics around software engineering and statistics.

Conclusion

What do you think? The last step in this section is to think about everything you've learned and decide what types of roles you're going to pursue. Keep in mind that you don't have to limit yourself to one segment forever- all we're doing is narrowing your focus initially so you'll be able to better connect with companies and increase your chances of getting a job offer for an exciting role.

Once you put yourself out there and refine your process, you'll learn more about the different roles and what might be best for you. This is an iterative process: you may start by pursuing Product Analyst roles, but then find that you're actually more interested in the sales side of analytics- then you can pursue a Sales Operations role.

Here's your formula:

1. Get clear on what the different segments are and what they mean: Data Analytics, Data Science, and Data Engineering.

2. Know yourself. Take the above assessment to find out which segment aligns with your interests and skills the most.

3. Dig deeper. Use the detailed breakdowns in this section to get a more thorough understanding of each segment and what different roles actually do.

4. Choose a path. Decide which path (and potentially which specific roles) you want to start pursuing. This will give you a specific focus and allow you to channel your energy in one direction. Don't worry- you can always re-calibrate later.

Think you can handle this? Hopefully this is exciting for you. This is a crucial first step in your journey in the world of data careers. By understanding exactly what you want, you'll not only be able to focus your studies and connect with the right opportunities, but you'll also feel better about your decision and avoid making the wrong career move. Read through this section a few times and get clear on what path is right for you.

Thoughts from a Hiring Manager:

"One of the main things I look for in candidates is: are they actually interested in this job specifically? Do they really want to do the work that my team does, or are they just interested in the title/company/something else? You'd be surprised at the number of candidates who, when I ask them what kind of work they're looking to do, they respond with something that's totally different than the job description.

If the role doesn't mention machine learning and the interviewer doesn't ask about it, then don't bring up machine learning. Better yet, if machine learning is where you're really passionate, go get one of those roles (there's plenty). I don't need someone who's good at everything- I need someone who is great at a few relevant things and will be happy with the work not just a week after being hired, but 6 months and a year after being hired. I want people who join my team to be fulfilled and successful long-term."

Self-Taught vs. Online Learning

Welcome to yet another step in your journey to break into the field of data. This is exciting because we're going to tackle one of the main questions people ask themselves when starting their journey to break into the field of data. It's good to ask this question as well- the people who don't end up doing as well in this field are the ones who get the idea they want to work in data, and immediately sign up for Udacity or some other online program. For them, when it gets tough, there's nothing motivating them to continue because they haven't thought about what they want exactly, and they haven't picked a method of learning that fits their goals.

This section is the perfect next step after you've read, "Choosing Your Path in Data", one of our other strategy sections. In, "Choosing Your Path" you'll have the tools to uncover exactly what path in data is right for you- some people are interested in pursuing Data Analyst and other analytics roles, while on the other end of the spectrum, some have the type of mind best suited to pursue Data Engineering roles. Whichever is the case for you, this section will be a fantastic resource to help you build the skills necessary to not only get those roles, but succeed in them. As we go through this material, we'll assume you've read the, "Choosing Your Path in Data" section and have a good idea of where you're heading.

The purpose of this section is to answer the age-old (sort of) question: Should I teach myself a certain set of skills, or should I take online classes? Because the data careers, and particularly Data Science, have become extremely popular only in the last few years, and online coursework hasn't been in the mainstream long either, no one has really tackled this question yet. Sure, you may find a few blog articles here and there, but there has been no long-form, detailed strategy section to really dig and and get the answer- until now.

This section will give you the framework to decipher whether you should focus mainly on looking for ways to teach yourself data skills (using books, online forums, articles, etc.), or if you should sign up for a full online course through a platform like Coursera. Once you understand your approach, you'll be able to move on to our other sections- for example, "Breakdown of Top 3 Online Learning Platforms" if you're going to online learning, or our "Essential Data Reading List". From there, you'll be able to dive in to the actual material.

Why This Chapter is Important

As you can tell by now, each section in our series is helping you build a strategy to ultimately get a fantastic job in the world of data, whether it's as a Data Analyst, Data Scientist, Data Engineer, or somewhere in between. This section is important because it's going to help you determine how you actually go about building the skills necessary. But why should we think about the "how"? Why not just save time and jump right in to a course or something, and then adjust later?

Many people feel that they should jump right into the material, and there's nothing wrong with poking around different data concepts to see what catches your eye. The problem is that you can spend a lot of time and a lot of money on something that isn't the best learning style for you, doesn't get you to your goals, is stressful rather than fun, and can leave you wondering why you're even doing it in the first place. A great strategy will set you on a path that is not only challenging, but interesting enough to get you through tough parts, and ultimately gets you to your goals. That is what we'll do in this section- let's dive in.

One of the most important things to think about initially is where you are and where you're going. "Where you are" essentially means your current level of skill working with data and how much you've worked with data in the past. There aren't hard and fast segments we can put you in, but here are a few potential groups:

Brand New

This category may fit you if you've never had a job where manipulating data was a part of your regular tasks. People in this category may have used data, whether it's in reporting, a spreadsheet, or something else, but have little to no experience analyzing or performing operations on the data. If you're not sure how to do formulas in Google Sheets or Excel, you're probably close to this category. Another good point of reference is your educational base- if your college major was something non-technical such as communications or English, it's another indicator that you might fall into this category (although recent experience is more relevant). If this is you, you may benefit from learning the basics in a well-structured online course.

Some Experience

Most job seekers looking to break into the field of data fall into this intermediate category, which describes those currently in a job that does some data work. This includes those in marketing roles who use Google Sheets or Excel to review lists and process results, and even certain sales roles have a small analytical element. This may also apply to you if you're working closely with Data Analysts or Data Scientists and have a birds-eye view of what their work looks like. This group has had a taste of the data world and wants more. If you can do basic formulas in spreadsheets, and consider yourself more analytically-minded, this is probably where you fit in. In terms of college experience you may or may not have had a more quantitative major, but regardless you likely gravitated toward technology and technical topics.

Already have a Role in Data

This is an interesting category because there are a lot of people who already have a role in data (typically as some sort of analyst) and want to move into something more advanced, or perhaps just do a similar role at a larger company that's difficult to get into. We see a lot of Marketing Analysts and Operations Analysts looking to become Data Scientists or Engineers at top tech company, and feel like they need help getting to the next step. If this is you, you'll know- generally if your day-to-day involves a lot of SQL querying and data manipulation, you have a data role. People in this bucket typically choose to teach themselves additional skills to move up to an advanced role, although it's not uncommon for them to take additional online coursework for topics that are very new to them.

These three buckets are a great guideline, but remember that this is a broad spectrum rather than a rigid classification. Where do you fit? Maybe you have some experience in data, but in terms of technical skills you pick things up quickly and are already moving on to move advanced topics such as SQL. Maybe you're doing a ton of data work and feel like you fit the "Already have a Role" bucket, but you don't have a technical title such as "Analyst" and your boss isn't technical either, so you feel like there are some gaps in your knowledge.

Next, we want to think about your outcome. If you've read our other sections, this is not new. Essentially we want to define what we're going after as our next move in the world of data, meaning the next role you're looking to enter. It doesn't have to be a long-term vision of where you want to be in five or ten years. All you need to do is define where you want to go next, and it starts with asking a few questions:

- What kind of work would I enjoy?

- What path in data is right for me (see our "Discover Your Path in Data" section)?

- What is a reasonable next step? Don't lower your sights, but also remember that there are certain roles that are very difficult to get and would require many years of work to even be considered.

- What type of company would I like to work at? Be flexible, but it's good to have some general guidelines.

Here's an example outcome: "My outcome is to have a fantastic role as a Data Analyst or Data Scientist where I tackle interesting problems at a top tech company"

One more: "My outcome is to break into the world of data by getting a great role within the Data Analyst path. I want to work at a company that is consumer-facing and mission-driven, and company size or prestige isn't as important to me."

What is your outcome? It doesn't have to be perfect, but go ahead and see what you can come up with. Make sure you write this down somewhere and don't just say it in your head- once you write things down they become more real, and many of the people who ultimately reach their outcome review it daily.

Last note on outcomes: they're flexible. You're not bound to anything when you write your outcome. We see many candidates who initially say they want to work at a startup, but after talking to lots of companies they decide they'd like to go for a more established company instead. The opposite also happens frequently. You need to define your outcome in the early stages of your job search, but don't be afraid to change it up if you want to go a different direction.

As you're thinking about where you currently stand in your data knowledge and what you want to achieve, the next logical consideration is the distance between the two. How big is the gap between where you are and where you want to be? If you're currently a Data Analyst at a mid-sized tech company and want to be a Data Scientist at a larger company, the gap probably isn't too big. If you're currently working as a server at a restaurant and want to be a Machine Learning Engineer, that's probably a bigger gap. The general rule of thumb is that it will take more time and formal education (eg. actual classes) if you have a large gap, but there are certainly exceptions. Keep in mind that you will learn more about the distance as you apply for jobs- for example, "Data Scientist" can mean lots of different things, and companies often have a spectrum of levels for their Data Scientists- meaning it's potentially easier to get in at a lower level and work your way up.

This is also a good time to think about if aiming for a stepping-stone role is right for you. In the restaurant server example above, although he can definitely work his way into an ML Engineer role eventually, they'd probably have an easier time starting as an analyst or entry-level Data Scientist, and then building up the skills along the way.

One of the important things we're doing in all of our sections is coming to an understanding of who you are as it relates to your career and abilities in data. Reflect on this. The better you understand where you stand, the easier it will be to pick an effective strategy to get you to your goals. Choose your outcome, know yourself, define a strategy, execute, improve, repeat. That's all there is to it.

Factors to consider

Naturally there are some factors to consider when you're thinking about which educational direction is right for you. The important thing to note here is that while you should definitely give these things some thought, don't suffer from "Analysis Paralysis": when you're analyzing so many different things that you get overwhelmed and never end up taking any action at all. Our recommendation is to spend a few hours (or less) analyzing the below, write down your thoughts, and then move on. Let's jump in.

Cost

This is something on everyone's mind when they think about how they're going to pursue education in the data field- how much is it going to cost? There are two truths: the first is that it can cost a lot of money if you choose, and the second is that it doesn't have to cost anything (financially) if you choose. Your reality will likely be somewhere in the middle- you'll spend a little money on great content that helps you grow, but it won't be crazy amounts. Let's look at each option and figure out the investment required.

Self-Taught

Contrary to popular belief, "Self-Taught" doesn't mean "Free" for most people, although it's certainly possible to learn everything you need to know with just an internet connection and a browser. It depends on the individual's learning style, but most people get a lot of value from books and similar non-course content.

We'll take a look at some resources in the "Essential Reading" section, but good books relating to data concepts tend to cost somewhere between $15-45. You shouldn't need many, but a budget of a $100 would go a long way to building up your resources. One note- it's a good idea to start with one book and see how you like learning that way. Some people love reading from a physical book, while others simply don't learn well that way and prefer some kind of video content. Don't spend a bunch of money on books before you know you like to learn that way.

Online Courses

Most people expect that online courses will cost money, but there is a lot of mystery and guessing around exactly how much. Truthfully, it depends on which platform (eg. Coursera, Udacity) you choose, as well as which program or programs you do.

Additionally, what many people don't understand at first is that the majority of online learning platforms have free options that allow you to take full course content without paying anything at all. What it usually comes down to is if you want an official certificate or credential that shows you've completed the material, and if so you'll need to pay anywhere from a few hundred to a few thousand dollars.

If you end up deciding that online learning is a viable path for you, check out our popular strategy deep dive: "Breakdown of Top 3 Online Platforms". There we go into detail about the program structure of Udacity, edX, and Coursera, and we reveal crucial info to know such as the program types, costs, and credentials available. Make sure you head over to that section before signing up for anything.

Time

Another important factor to consider is how much time you want to spend learning before you're ready to look for a new job. This will play a big part in helping you determine which learning method to choose, because one path won't necessarily work for a given time constraint.

For example, if you have some good experience and want to start looking for new roles in a month, you probably won't want to sign up for a big online course. In that case you'd probably want to go the self-taught route and dig into the skills you need to build up.

On the other hand, if you're less constrained on time and are looking to be in a new role between six months to a year from now, you have more options. Even if you're already experienced in data, you may benefit from the structure and comprehensive coursework of a full online program, particularly if you're looking to enter a new field within data (eg. Data Engineering).

Credential

Whether or not you need a credential can vary on a lot of things, primarily what your education and work experience looks like. Many who work in a role that is far away from their goal, such as a server or some sort of blue-collar work feel that they need to get a degree or credential of some kind to make the leap to the corporate world, and that's often a good idea. In this case, online learning is probably the way to go since self-teaching obviously doesn't have any certification component.

Others have a good quantitative degree, and potentially even an advanced degree, and also have relevant work experience in data. For them, continuing education in order to pursue a new role is simply a matter of beefing up their skills so they can get qualified and do well in interviews. For these job-seekers, self-teaching is a more efficient way to reach their ultimate outcome.

Based on initial research for this strategy guide, most people fall somewhere in the middle. They are already in the corporate world, and have had some taste of data work, although they're not in a full data role yet. Their decision isn't as cut and dry as the above two examples, but many of them tend to lean more toward online coursework for the credentialing aspect because it gives them a great base of foundational knowledge, and the credential can't hurt.

For a more in-depth analysis on the topic of credentialing, take a look at our "Breakdown of Top 3 Online Learning Platforms" section. There we get into detail about the different types of credentials available and also dig into whether or not you actually need a verifiable certificate.

Current Position and Mobility

One of the important things many people forget to factor into their decision when looking to pursue a career in data is where they stand at their current employer and what the opportunities look like. One of the smartest things you can do, if at all possible, is to move into a data role within your current employer and learn on the job. We'll go ahead and lump this into the "self-taught" bucket, but in reality you'll be learning a lot from your environment and the people around you.

Here's an example: let's say you're a marketing coordinator at a small tech company and have been there for a year and a half. Assuming you're on good terms with your boss and the company itself, you can have a conversation about how you ultimately want to pursue data-driven roles, and would love to do it in your current company. If you see current job openings at your company, all the better. What many early-career people don't realize is that it's really expensive to hire from the outside, and there's a lot of uncertainty involved. Faced with the decision, most companies would rather move someone they know is reliable into a different role than let them leave the company and have to hire someone external for the role (not to mention backfilling the role the person left).

There is some nuance to this conversation, however. You can't just pull your boss aside and say you're going to quit if you can't move into an analyst role (for example). People don't like to be threatened, and it won't go well. What you can do is have an honest conversation about how you're passionate about working with data, are doing lots of work to learn things on your own, and ask their advice about how you could pursue something within the company. You want to be pleasant and don't make it seem like you're going to quit. Just let them know it's something you're working toward and would love the opportunity to do a role at your current company.

The pros of this approach are that you (should) already have a good reputation at your current company, which will make them more likely to want to move you. It's also likely that you won't be competing with as many people as you would on the open job market, or at least you'd have an advantage over them because you're a known quantity at your company.

The major con is that you'll almost certainly make less money than if you moved to the same role at a different company. Internal processes within companies can be quite rigid, and many won't do big pay increases, even if you enter a completely new role. That said, one great strategy is to move into a new, data-driven role at your current company if you can, and then later move to a different company after you've accumulated some experience and accomplishments for your resume. It's much easier to get a data role if you're already in a data role.

In summary, if you can move to a data role within your current company, you'll be able to learn a lot on the job and probably won't have to take a full online program. If this seems possible for you, go ahead and have that conversation with your boss and see what the options are. If it doesn't seem realistic because of your position (eg. you work at a restaurant), or your boss tells you it's not possible, an online program can be a great way to stick out in the job pool.

The Ideal Way to Learn

The last topic we'll go into has less to do with your background. Now we want to think about what your learning style is and how you'd do with the mediums we're discussing here. Think about your past- have you had success watching video courses online (for any subject), or have you done the best reading books and digging into things yourself? Remember that each way of learning has unique benefits: on the online learning side, for example, many people feel that the deadlines built into the program help them continue to move forward and push themselves to grow. On the other side, self-teaching allows you to take in a broad array of perspectives on topics and see other points of view- which can lead to a deeper understanding of the concepts.

Most people have some experience with both and can probably do OK with either learning style, but at the same time they tend to lean one way over the other. The easiest way for you to understand how online platforms or self-teaching work for you is to give them each a try. Remember that you don't have to fully commit to any learning program or any method at the beginning- you can and should "shop around" and see what suits you. We've got some great resources in our "Essential Data Reading List", and some of them are totally free and open-source. Definitely check those out. You can also look through our "Breakdown of Top 3 Online Learning Platforms" section and see what you can try out for free.

Once you get an idea of your learning style and what works best for you, you'll be able to add that to your evaluation process and choose the best path forward. Before you know it, you'll be on your way to an amazing and enjoyable career in data.

Final words

We're going to close this section out with a few final tips and words of advice. First of all, don't get overwhelmed by the choice between online learning and self-teaching. Even if you get it wrong and sign up for an online course that's not perfect for your needs, you can always remedy the situation by signing up for a different program or teaching yourself the skills you need.

On a similar note, know that it doesn't have to be one or the other. In this section we've been focused on getting you started on the right path so you can start making progress toward your goals as soon as possible. But this is just a starting place. Many people find themselves starting with one learning method, and then switching back and forth over time as they look for both wider and deeper knowledge in the field of data.

For example, one learner recently started by self-teaching basic concepts in Python and SQL, and applying them in his current job as much as possible. After some time, he realized that it would be hard to teach himself statistical concepts he needed to pursue a role in Data Science, so he took a full online program through Coursera. After a lot of work, this ultimately led to him getting a great role as a Data Scientist in a large, pre-IPO tech company. This is possible for you too.

Also keep in mind that whatever you skills and concepts you can apply in a business context will be most beneficial for your learning and for when you start interviewing. If at all possible, you want to apply what you're learning to your current role, even if it's extra stuff on top of your day job. Above we mentioned having a conversation with your manager about how you're looking to pursue a role in data, and you can also reach out to Data Analysts, Data Scientists, and Data Engineers within your company to learn about what they do and how you might apply it. When you use this approach, you don't have to narrowly focus on people in the same exact path you're ultimately pursuing (eg. Data Engineering). Feel free to meet and interact with anyone in the field of data- understanding all the different roles and how they work will benefit you greatly, because no one in any data roles works in a vacuum.

If you're not currently working, or it isn't possible to apply data skills to your current job, work on projects that have a business context or application. Most data education programs have a project component, where you put together a larger piece of work on your own (very common in programs that have a Machine Learning element). One mistake that many learners make is that they're not thoughtful about the type of project they do, and it ultimately doesn't resonate with the recruiter or hiring manager.

For example, there is a classic dataset with types of Irises (a flower), and a popular Machine Learning project is to build a model to predict the type of Iris given the features of a plant. This is great if you plan to go into horticulture, but it's unlikely to be impactful with a hiring team. What's the business application of the model? How does it apply to real-world problems?

As an exercise, let's take a look at three potential projects, all of which are possible via open-sourced datasets:

1. Predicting the type of Iris (Iris dataset)

2. Predicting neighborhoods in Brooklyn where crimes are most likely to occur in the future (Brooklyn Crime dataset)

3. Predicting user demand on Airbnb to determine the key markets for supply acquisition (Airbnb dataset)

Of these, which do you think would resonate most with a recruiter or hiring manager? We can safely exclude #1, as we already described. #2 is better, and probably more interesting- since police departments function as a business in many ways, you can add some "business" context into your project by talking about where you would invest resources to prevent future crimes. #3 is our best bet, since it is similar to real-world problems that a company would face. When you do this kind of project, you have the opportunity to create a plan describing the business problem, ideal outcome, and how you will get there using data.

Remember that hiring teams aren't going to have the time to look through all of your projects, and in all likelihood they're going to just skim one of them. Put your best and most interesting project first, and make sure it's one that applies to the business world. If you're not sure where to start, we recommend first compiling a list of datasets and APIs you can pull data from- go for well-known companies like Uber, Twitter, and Airbnb. Once you have your list of datasets and companies, do research on the problems and challenges these specific companies are facing. What is the biggest roadblock for Twitter right now? Is it fraud or abusive content? Does Uber trying to get more drivers or more passengers? Jot down a few bullet points about the challenges you're finding, and then link the source (usually a news article). When you create your project, you can even link to these articles to show that the problem you're solving is a real one. The last step before diving in is to check the datasets to make sure that the data available can be used to solve the problem. For example, if the Uber datasets or API doesn't have information on drivers, it would be hard to solve a problem on driver growth.

Once you have that figured out, go ahead and start your project. This isn't meant to be a guide on how to make a Data project for your portfolio, but hopefully this information points you in the right direction. Remember: when it comes to portfolios and projects, the more business relevance a project has, the better. Go for the ideas that are both interesting to you and can solve a real-world business problem (or at least a problem that could be real). This kind of project will have a bigger impact on the hiring team and increase your chances of success.

This is it. By now you've gotten an idea of the paths available to you and are probably starting to lean in the direction of either self-taught or online learning. Remember that it's important to think about this before your commit to something fully, but this isn't a forever decision- if you decide to self-teach for a few months and then move to an online program, you'll still be in great shape. In fact, most people see the choice between self-teaching and online learning not as "one or the other" but as a question of, "Where should I start?". Using that frame, the choice becomes easier. As a next step, go through this section and write down your thoughts. What are your decision points? Where do you fall into the buckets we described? What is available to you in your current role? As you review the information and write down your thoughts, the decision will become more clear. Additionally, if you'd like more detail on online programs, you can use the chapter: "Breakdown of the Top 3 Online Learning Platforms". There we have a breakdown of Udacity, edX, and Coursera, and go deep into the details about the coursework itself, costs associated, and credentialing opportunities.

Top 3 Online Learning Platforms: Dissected

The purpose of this section is to give you an understanding of the Top 3 Online Learning platforms: Coursera, edX, and Udacity. This is not going to be like the free articles you see everywhere that claim to compare the three, and sometimes even try to give them a "score", but by then end of the article the writer just, "But really it's up to your learning style". We're going to go deep. We're going to actually figure out which platform is right for you, and you'll leave this section with a good idea of where to start.

Keep in mind, online classes aren't the best for everyone. In fact, we have another section called "Self Taught vs. Online Classes: The Ultimate Guide" that helps you figure out which path is right for you. This section assumes that you've already read "Self-Taught vs. Online Classes: The Ultimate Guide" and have decided that online learning is best for you. All of that said, online classes are a great tool to beef up your data skills, and even if it's not the end-all-be-all, you'll probably find yourself taking courses at some point, even if it's just to supplement your self-study.

Let's begin by thinking about the outcome for you taking the course. Naturally everyone wants to learn, but there are other factors as well that need to be weighed, which will ultimately affect your decision. Here are some things to consider:

What type of role are you interested in? What path in data is best for you? If you're not sure, try reading (or re-reading) the chapter, "Discover Your Path in Data" and find roles that are right for you.

What is your current level of skill? Are you starting from scratch, or do you have some experience writing SQL, Python, doing data analysis, maybe even statistics, etc? Most platforms have options for all levels, but it's good to think about where you stand as you evaluate different resources.

Are you looking to get a credential or certificate of some sort, or is just the knowledge enough for you? If you're interested in a credential, is there additional value to you in having a University attached to it? Most candidates are interested in having something certifiable to show that they've completed the course and learned the material.

How much are you willing to invest in a course? Don't worry if you're not able to invest a lot- most people can't. There are free and low-priced options for educating yourself online. If you do have a budget, however, more power to you, and you may be able to get more of the "premium" learning experiences.

Going back to the idea of your outcome, what is yours? We want to get specific here, and make it exciting. "I want to learn data science" is not a good outcome. First of all, it's not specific enough for you to understand when you've achieved the outcome. How do you know when you've "learned data science"? We can do better than that.

How about, "My outcome is to develop skills in data science that enable me to get a role as a Data Scientist at a tech company. In particular, I want to focus on machine learning and be competent at producing useful models." This is much better because it's exact enough to let you know where you stand. You can take some time to aggregate job postings for data scientists and list out the skills you see come up regularly, then self-assess as you learn new concepts. For example, maybe "linear regression" is listed on several Data Scientist role postings, so you can work on that skill and evaluate yourself.

Our second version is good, but it still needs a little work. It needs to be more inspiring. Language is very impactful for us, and having a juicy outcome will push you to do better than your best and will motivate you to navigate through setbacks. Remember this: what you say matters, and how you say it matters. We've covered the what (be specific, etc.), and now we're going to work on the "how to say it".

Try saying this outcome out loud, with lots of energy: "My outcome is to create and cultivate top-level skills that help me get a fantastic job as a Data Scientist at a great company where I'd be excited to come into work every day."

Isn't that sexier than, "I want to learn data science"? You bet it is. This is the kind of outcome that inspires and motivates you to do incredible work and improve yourself at a lightening-fast rate. This is the kind of outcome that gets you to jump out of bed at 4am on Saturday with a huge smile on your face, ready to take on the world and get to work on your skills. This is the type of outcome that makes you hungry for knowledge. This outcome gives you drive. When it comes to taking online classes, everyone has moments when they don't want to watch the lecture, don't want to take notes, don't want to do the assignment right now, etc. Everyone has moments where they'd rather watch TV or go get something to eat or hang out with friends. When this happens to you and you're feeling demotivated, a juicy outcome will pump you up and get you back in the zone to do great work.

Now, write out your outcome. Make it specific, and make it interesting. Make it juicy. This is going to carry you through the inevitable challenges that arise when you're trying to break into a new field. Your outcome is essentially a reminder to yourself of what, exactly, you want, and it will help you understand if you're heading in the right direction or not. Keep in mind, it's flexible too- for example, you may initially write as a part of your outcome that you want to work at a top 10 tech company, but later discover that you're actually interested in the idea of a smaller company, in which case it's absolutely fine to update your outcome. Know where you're going, and be flexible in your approach. This is going to be your North Star.

Now, we can get to the meat of this section: understanding the top 3 online learning platforms and helping you understand which one will best help you reach your outcome. It is important to think about this up front, before you invest time and money because you want to ensure that you're making the most of your resources (again, time and money). Make sure to read this section all the way through before starting a course or putting in your credit card info anywhere.

We're going to evaluate these platforms using 3 Cs: Coursework, Credentialing, and Cost. Sections on Coursework will help you understand what types of things you can learn on the given platform, which is a major factor in choosing which direction to go. Credentialing will cover what sort of certifications are available. All of these platforms offer some sort of credential, but they vary in subtle ways that can impact your path (if credentialing is an important factor to you).

We'll also cover costs and give you a good idea of what sort of investment is required, if any. The price structure for most online education platforms is usually that courses are free to try or perhaps fully audit, but paying unlocks premium content and credentials/certificates. The good news is that you can learn almost anything for free online, so there are options for every budget, including $0. At this point, cost should be the least of your concerns, but we'll make sure to get you fully up to speed.

We'll be sure to point out any subtle differences between the platforms and try to give you an understanding of what the user experience will be like. Additionally, after we go over each platform in detail, we'll dissect factors like cost and credentialing further to answer questions like, "Do I even need an official certificate?" Again, make sure to read through this entire section before making a decision and moving forward with an online learning platform. Let's begin.

Udacity

udacity.com

Udacity was founded in 2011 by Sebastian Thrun, a former Vice President at Google and Professor of Computer Science at Stanford. Depending on your age, you may remember that back in 2011 Stanford open-sourced some of its courses in Computer Science, and those courses were actually the starting point for Udacity. Here's their mission statement: "Our mission is to democratize education through the offering of world-class higher education opportunities that are accessible, flexible, and economical."

Udacity is a great platform and definitely one of the most popular among online learners, even those who traditionally have self-taught.

Coursework

Udacity has a great deal of coursework available, neatly organized into categories like, "Data Science" or, "Artificial Intelligence". Interestingly, within categories, the coursework is sometimes subdivided into job titles such as "Data Analyst" or "Data Engineer", which are often referring to Udacity's Nanodegrees, which are just what the name implies- small versions of degrees that focus on one particular skillset (e.g. Data Analytics) and have several courses teaching different concepts.

Outside of the bread-and-butter coursework for something like a Data Analyst path, Udacity offers other interesting subjects for study. For example, they have a great body of classes on Autonomous Systems, including coursework on Self-Driving technology and Robotics. For someone who already has a great technical base and is looking to branch into more advanced coursework, there are a lot of compelling options.

Additionally there are some courses available to help you along with your career, including a class called, "Applying for Jobs", and one called, "Interviewing". Since you should already have our other section, "6 Figures in 60 Days: The Ultimate Strategy", you should be OK on this topic, but some people feel more comfortable supplementing their knowledge and hearing another voice. If that describes you, feel free to make use of these Udacity offerings, but keep in mind that early in your journey you want to establish a solid foundation of technical and problem-solving skills, which means your time is best spent learning the ins and outs of how to work with data effectively.

Overall, Udacity has a great body of coursework, but is somewhat limited compared to other platforms (meaning there are fewer course options). One interesting part of Udacity is that there tends to be just one course (or very few) on a specific topic. For example, there's just one course on Data Visualization with Python. As we'll see later in this chapter, other platforms often offer multiple courses on the same (or similar) subjects, usually with a different teacher. This tells us that Udacity has taken a curated approach to creating their catalog, which has its pros and cons.

The upsides of this approach include the fact that it's much easier to choose coursework on Udacity than other platforms, if you've already determined what path is right for you. For example, let's say you want to ultimately be a Data Engineer- there's basically one choice on Udacity: the Data Engineer Nanodegree. This is a benefit for most people because many get lost in, "analysis paralysis", which is when you have so many options that you're just overwhelmed and don't end up choosing anything at all. That is not a place you want to be (trust me).

The downsides of having one or few options is that there really isn't a way to re-adjust if you're not getting in sync with the instructor or the way the material is presented. As you surely remember from high school, different teachers work better or worse with different students, and a lot of it comes down to the style of the teacher and how they arrange the coursework. That said, this shouldn't be a major concern, for two reasons: 1. Udacity offers a refund if you cancel within the first 7 days of starting a Nanodegree, and 2. Instructors on this and other top platforms are vetted and have shown that they can effectively teach the material. When using a major online learning platform like Udacity, most people find they succeed if they put in the time and effort to do well.

Credentialing

Now, let's get into the credentialing/certification options available. Udacity has carved out its own place in this space through "Nanodegree" programs. A Nanodegree is an earned credential signifying that you've met a certain standard of learning set forth by the Nanodegree program. This is the same idea as other certificates that exist, such as the PMP certification for project managers (Project Management Professional) or Six Sigma certification for those involved in improving business processes.

Some platforms offer certificates for single courses, but Nanodegrees are earned only through completion of an entire set of coursework. For example, in order to earn a Nanodegree in Data Science, you'd have to complete all of the courses in the Data Scientist program. This is great for learners who aren't already familiar with exactly what subject matter they need to learn.

Cost

First, let's get an understanding of the free options available to you Udacity, as well as the limitations of the free options. Udacity offers a number of full courses free-of-charge, and there are some very useful ones such as, "Intro to Relational Databases" and "A/B Testing" (statistics). These are great for brushing up on foundational concepts or specific skills that complement other learning material.

The downside of these free courses is that there's not really a logical learning structure the course fits into. In the example of the A/B Testing course, you can definitely take it and learn useful material, but how do you know where it fits into the grand scheme of your potential role? Is it even information you need to focus on for your specific path in data and the roles you're applying to? Knowing about A/B testing certainly wouldn't hurt, but there are a lot of data roles that don't need to have an in-depth knowledge of how to execute these tasks.

Additionally, most of the coursework with the Nanodegree learning programs isn't offered for free. For example, signing up for the Data Engineer Nanodegree and paying the monthly fee will unlock lots of great courses and content that just isn't accessible for free. One of the main advantages of full online learning programs, as opposed to just one-off courses, is that you're learning something end-to-end, and thinks link together in a coherent way. You start out with foundational information, ie. things you need to know that make it possible to learn everything else. Then, you get into more specific information, but you do so in a fluid way- everything connects and it helps your comprehension dramatically.

If you're looking to brush up on some specific skills, and Udacity has a course on that subject, go ahead and stick with the free version. If you're looking for something more complete and comprehensive, you'll probably want to go with the paid Nanodegree programs or choose a different platform.

Before we move on to a detailed explanation of the paid programs Udacity offers, there's one thing we should call out- the, "Career Advancement" courses. These are video lectures that aren't focused on the technical side of being a professional in data- instead, these courses deal with soft skills that are essential to being successful in any data path long-term. Regardless of where you are in your career, you should definitely go through the courses related to interviews if you're looking for a new job (eg., "Data Science Interviews"). We'll give you some great advice in these chapters, and there are plenty of resources out there, but definitely check these out too.

The costs associated with learning programs on Udacity are fairly straightforward. For a Nanodegree, the cost as of this writing is $399 per month, and programs range from 2-6 months in length. There is also the option of paying up-front for the coursework and getting a decent discount. Here's the current cost breakdowns for the three paths we've discussed in this book:

Data Analyst (est. 4 months): \$399/mo = \$1,596 total, or \$1,436 if paid up front.

Data Scientist (est. 4 months): \$399/mo = \$1,596 total, or \$1,436 if paid up front.

Data Engineer (est. 5 months): \$399/mo = \$1,995 total, or \$1,795 if paid up front.

As you can see, there's the opportunity to save a little money if you decide to pay up front. Before you charge your credit card, there's something you should keep in mind: no matter what the estimated program length is, you don't have to pay once you're done with the curriculum.

For example, let's say you start the Data Scientist program and work your tail off to finish in 2.5 months. You would only pay for 3 months (you're billed on the first and there's no partial-month billing), which would come to a total of \$1,197 (\$399 * 3). This obviously beats the discount price. The other thing to note is that even if you do the "paid up front" option, you'll only get access for the number of months they estimate it will take you to finish the curriculum, and if you need more time you'll have to start paying \$399 per month. In other words, paying up front isn't a way to insure that you'll get a lower rate if you need more time to finish.

If you're the type of person who is going to work like crazy on the online courses and really spend time focused on learning the material, it's probably better to go with the monthly payments and see if you can finish early. On the other hand, if you lots of other obligations that mean you won't be able to give this a ton of time, and think that you'll probably complete the courses in the estimated time or longer, you might want to go ahead and pay up front.

That said, if you're unsure about where you stand, we recommend paying monthly and really giving this your best effort. $399 is a big chunk of money for most people, and seeing that CC charge every month should motivate you to work hard and push through the coursework to completion.

Lastly in this section, we want to remind you should take your time to think about your options before investing in online coursework. You need to understand what path you're going to take, what skills you have, what skills you need, and how important the credentialing aspect is to you. We're going to address some of the nuance here in later sections, but don't let these numbers make you too nervous or get you too excited- be patient and try to figure out what's right for you. Udacity and other online learning platforms are fantastic resources, and they're often even better when you pay for premium versions, but remember that you don't have to invest a lot of money (or any money) into learning these skills to be successful. Just about anything can be learned online for free, and ultimately what will get you a great role and move your career forward are real skills to do the work.

edX

edX.org

Another popular online learning platform is edX, which was founded in 2012 by the Massachusetts Institute of Technology (M.I.T.) and Harvard University. EdX has goals similar to Udacity, but one of the key differences is that all of the course content is provided by actual universities and higher-education institutions. Does this matter? Maybe, maybe not, but it might be beneficial to receive instruction from people who have been teaching for a long time and have plenty of practice communicating the concepts. Also, there is the fact that you can attach the name of the institution when you put your coursework on your resume, but we'll go over that in more detail in the, "Credentialing" section.

Also, know that edX is a non-profit (hence the .org domain name). This probably doesn't mean much in practice, but some people feel better taking classes through non-profit organizations over for-profit companies.

Coursework

EdX coursework is largely provided by the institutions themselves. One of the interesting features of edX coursework is that they offer much more subject matter variety than platforms like Udacity, which focus on technical skills. EdX has a multitude of offerings in not only Data and Computer Science, but also subjects like Entrepreneurship, Chemistry, Math, and Medicine (and many more).

But you want to learn about data and acquire the skills to get you a fantastic new role, so does this matter? For most, no, but for people who are in no rush to move into a new career path and want to build foundational, theory-level skills, courses like "Fundamentals of Statistics", "Statistical Thinking for Data Science", or "Essential Math for Machine Learning" could be really useful.

Either way, you can still leverage the courses in Data on edX to help you achieve your goals. EdX actually has more ways than most major platforms to learn important material: individual courses, Professional Certificates, MicroMasters, Online Master's, and XSeries. What do all of these mean? Let's look at short descriptions of each and make the picture clear.

Individual Courses: Pretty self-explanatory. These come in many different flavors, with courses such as "Data Science: Visualization", or "Python Basics for Data Science". Most of the courses allow you to take them for free, and pay extra if you'd like to have your assignments graded and receive an official certificate of completion. This is a major advantage over Udacity, which does offer some free courses, but likely not as much as most people are looking for.

Professional Certificates: These are interesting groups of coursework that are comprised of several related courses that combine nicely to build your skills in a certain area. One good example is the, "Microsoft Professional Program in Artificial Intelligence" (created by Microsoft, of course). These are nice because you'll get a more coherent body of information than you would semi-randomly selecting courses. The downside is that these tend to be pretty narrow in focus, so if you're looking to build a more end-to-end skillset it may be better to go with a different option. You can take individual courses for free, or pay per course and get the certifiable certificate.

MicroMasters: As you can see, the good people at edX are quite creative with their program creation. Jokes aside, a MicroMasters could be an interesting route for someone looking to get into the field of data and may want to get a Master's degree in the future. Essentially a MicroMasters is a group of connected courses that are the fundamental courses you would take in a Master's program. The MicroMasters stands on its own like any other certificate, and if you choose to go for a full Master's degree in the future you can get those course credits applied to your degree (you won't have to pay for them again or take the courses again). For example, you could sign up for the MicroMasters program in Data Science from the University of San Diego, and then later get your full Master's in Data Science. Make sure you read the fine print if you're going to pursue this route, however, because MicroMasters coursework for a given program only applies to one (or a select few) universities.

MicroMaster programs will take a bit longer than other certificates, and edX estimates around 1 year to complete the full program.

Online Master's Degrees: We're seeing a somewhat new area emerge in the world of online learning- true Master's Degrees, fully online. Curriculum-wise these are no different than a Master's you would earn by attending a university on-campus, but there are a few key advantages: they're fully online, they're somewhat self-paced in that you can take however many classes per semester that fit into your schedule, and they often cost less than a traditional on-campus program. These are the most in-depth option into the subject matter and will likely take students 1-3 years to complete, depending on your course load. We'll talk more about credentialing in the next section, but as you can imagine, a Master's degree makes it easy for recruiters and hiring managers to understand your level of knowledge. Note that these are actual degrees offered by universities such as Georgia Tech and the University of Texas, so you would have a degree from the university, not edX.

XSeries: Yes, another program type offered by edX. Once again these are sponsored by institutions, and the main difference is these are a bit more focused on the application of skills to a particular field or industry, and are generally more in-depth than other course offerings. For example, one program is called, "Data Analysis for Life Sciences". Other than that, the format is fairly similar, with the programs usually having around four courses and estimated to take 4-6 months of effort. As of this writing, XSeries is the most limited option with fewer than five programs focused on data, so it may be best to go with one of the above options.

So, what should you pick? Again, don't sign up for anything until you've read this section in full, but by now you're probably getting an idea of what's right for you. Most people, regardless of their work experience, find that program-based online learning helps them move closer to their goal of getting a great job in data than taking individual courses, which are usually better suited for people who are already in a data-driven role and want to beef up their skills.

Another important consideration is the time you're willing to spend on coursework. Do you want to take a few years and get your Master's? What about one year? Many people want to spend just a few months on a program, get out in the job market, land a job, and then improve their skills from there. Keep in mind that a longer program isn't necessarily better and won't necessarily get you a better job.

Credentialing

Thankfully, edX credentials are somewhat easier to understand than the program structure itself. You have a lot of options, so when it comes to credentials it's best to think about them in terms of four buckets: Professional Certificates, MicroMasters, Master's Degrees, and no credential at all. Let's look at each one in detail.

Profession Certificates are offered at just about every online learning platform that exists, and edX is no different. One interesting contrast between edX and

Udacity is that, with edX, you can get a certificate for a single course, whereas with Udacity the only certification comes with taking a full Nanodegree. Most learners pursue fuller program-time online education, but this is something to be aware of.

Another interesting distinction with edX compared to many other platforms is that the content is sponsored by a university or institution, rather than the platform itself-meaning, of course, that you'd have a certificate that looks something like, "Professional Certificate in Data Science from Harvard" rather than, "from edX" (although certificates themselves are co-branded with both the sponsoring institution and edX.

Why is this an important distinction? Many believe that having a university brand on a resume carries a bit more weight than just an online learning platform, since it's possible that there is still some stigma around online learning, and it's almost certainly true that a top university wouldn't risk its reputation with educational material of sub-par value. Plus, if the course content came from a university like Harvard or Berkeley, it's easier for recruiters and hiring managers to trust the quality of what you were taught. Think about it- if you have a Professional Certificate in Data Science from Harvard, as a hiring manager I would have more confidence in that educational material than an online platform without the same reputation. If you had a certificate from Never-heard-of-it.com, the hiring manager wouldn't have a clue if you'd been taught that 2 + 2 = 5 or the sky is green, or worse. The general recommendation we give to people is to go for online learning programs that have the content created by universities or reputable companies, rather than the platforms themselves.

MicroMasters are the next evolution of online learning. For these, obviously you'll need to take an entire program to get the credential, rather than just a single course, and naturally these are sponsored by universities and other educational institutions. As we mentioned before, these are fantastic if you're interested in getting a Master's degree at some point but don't want to make the full leap just yet, but the question remains of whether these are a "better" credential than a Professional Certificate.

Opinions are mixed. On the one hand, some people (including some hiring managers and recruiters) see no difference, since both program types involve online learning and likely have similar content. On the other hand, some people perceive a MicroMasters as more valuable since the courses are true graduate-level courses and apply toward a Master's degree at the given institution. In other words, it goes without saying that these classes aren't a walk in the park. In the end, the choice of Professional Certificate vs. MicroMasters will come down to what kind of information you want to learn (there are generally more options in the Professional Certificate group), what kind of time and financial commitment you're willing to make, and what you think the future holds for you and the type of education you want to pursue.

The last program type we'll discuss in the Credential section is also the easiest for everyone to understand: the Master's Degree. On edX, Master's degrees are just that- a Master's in the program of study from the given institution. These degrees should pass any educational background check and won't look any different than if you got your Master's on campus. For most learners and job seekers, it's a no-brainer that they'd prefer to get a Master's degree than anything else, and it's probably true that it holds more weight than any other certification. In the wide, wide world of credentialing, the Master's wins, but more often than not people chose to pursue a different route for two main reasons: time and cost. We've already talked about the time commitment in the above section describing the coursework, and we'll talk about cost in the next section. Just know that if you're looking to invest a few years and $10k+ on education in the data world, a Master's degree is probably right for you, and edX has some great ones to choose from.

Thoughts from a Hiring Manager:

"I don't know a lot about online programs or the differences between them. The reason I think completing online coursework is great is it shows me the person is committed to improving themselves and willing to put in the work to get better. On the other hand, I also know that online learning has its disadvantages, and a certificate or something is no guarantee the candidate actually knows the information. Of course I would give a candidate with online learning the same technical and business case questions I give everyone, and really try to get a thorough understanding of what they can do and how well they'd fit into the role."

My advice for anyone looking to pursue online learning is to do it for the right reasons: namely, that you want to learn skills to do great work. The wrong reason would be that you want a credential on your resume. The credential may get you interviews at some companies, but a credential alone won't get you a job, and it certainly won't make you successful once you do get a job.

Cost

At last, the question that's probably been on your mind while reading this section: how much does all this cost? It varies by the type of program. In general edX online programs are less expensive than Udacity's, which (combined with the university name brands) makes for a compelling offer for those looking to break into the data world.

One other important point of comparison is the availability of the materials as it relates to the cost. As we saw in the last section, Udacity's Nanodegree programs require a paid monthly subscription to not only receive the official certificate, but also to access the material at all. Many people love edX because they can access the course material for free, and only if they want a verified certificate do they have to pay anything. Not that this is true for a large majority of the coursework on edX, but curriculum in the Online Master's programs will likely not be available.

Here's a closer look at the costs for the programs mentioned:

Individual courses: Once again, these are fairly limited in scope but can be great resources for digging into a specific topic. For example, "Essential Math for Machine Learning: Python Edition" is currently offered through Microsoft, and would be very useful for those looking to pursue Data Science roles involving algorithms and machine learning. If you'd like a verified certificate, the cost is $99.

Professional Certificate: The next level up, the Professional Certificate, involves much more comprehensive coursework and essentially strings together relevant material that will help you build holistic skills in a given area. Another offering from Microsoft is the, "Microsoft Professional Program in Data Science". This has ten courses and a capstone project (which counts as a course), and you can get the official program certificate for $99 per course, or $1,089. As of the time of this writing there doesn't appear to be a discount for purchasing the whole program. Most other Professional Certificates are in this price range, with individual courses typically costing $99.

MicroMasters: This is where the cost structure starts to change a bit. The price will depend on the program and university, but for something in a data career path you can expect to pay somewhere between $1,000-$1,500 for four courses. Note that while there are far fewer classes to take, these real, graduate-level courses with plenty of substance to challenge you and help you grow. Another thing to note is that, while you can buy these courses individually, some programs do give you a discount for purchasing the whole MicroMasters at once. For example, the University of San Diego Data Science MicroMasters currently costs $350 for individual courses, but if you the whole program together (4 courses), you only pay $1,260, which saves you $___ (you do the calculation- you're in the data world now).

It's worth pointing out that MicroMasters are interesting because, while they aren't technically college credit, they can be applied to a Master's degree in the future, which makes them a lot more valuable for those who want to pursue even higher education later on.

Online Master's Degrees: Pull your wallet out for this one- an online Master's through edX will cost you somewhere from $9,000-$15,000, depending on which data program you choose. While the cost here is definitely a long way from the Professional Certificates and even MicroMasters, many people (including recruiters and hiring managers) believe that this is the most legitimate and comprehensive form of online learning. It's certainly worth considering, but remember that plenty of people have outstanding careers in data without a postgraduate degree, and at even some of the most prestigious tech companies you're likely to find that the majority of successful data analysts, scientists, and engineers don't have a Master's.

All of that said, consider it. If this is an area where you're willing to invest the time and money required to get a Master's, you'll probably enjoy it and learn an incredible amount of useful information and skills that will put you on the path to long-term success.

XSeries: In the final program offering, we're circling back to the first pricing model we saw: roughly $99 per course. XSeries clock in at 3-4 courses, so you're looking at $300-$400 for a certificate. The selection for edX's XSeries programs is quite limited, and in conversations with both people looking to break into data and those already in the field who want to improve their skills we've found that there's not as much interest in XSeries. Take a look at the courses for yourself and see if any of the programs make sense for your goals.

coursera

Coursera

coursera.com

Coursera is another major online learning platform that is an offshoot of online coursework at Stanford, founded by former professors Andrew Ng and Daphne Koller. If you've done the research on online learning in the data world before, you've probably heard of founder Andrew Ng- his seminal online course in Machine Learning is widely considered as one of the most important efforts in the establishment of online learning as a legitimate way to build crucial job skills.

Coursera is a massive platform, and as of this writing over 40 million people have taken courses here. Undoubtedly you've explored or at least heard about this platform before, so let's get into the details and see if it makes sense for you.

Coursework

Like edX, coursework on Coursera is backed by universities and other institutions. The University of Michigan, Johns Hopkins, IBM, and many international universities are among the institutions that create and support course content. If you decide to pursue a program through Coursera, you'll find that the majority of the classes are taught by professors or other leaders at the institutions themselves.

What's impressive and really stands out about Coursera is the breadth and depth of offerings available in the data world, and while browsing through the site you definitely get the feeling that it's a data-oriented platform. In addition to straightforward programs such as, "Data Science" (by Johns Hopkins), there are also deep dives into fascinating topics, such as the "Deep Learning Specialization", offered by deeplearning.ai, a company that has made it its mission to make education in Artificial Intelligence available to people around the world.

Fortunately, Coursera has taken a more simplified approach to program types than edX, but has a little more flexibility than Udacity. Let's dig into each offering and get to know the intricacies.

Individual Courses: Like our other platforms, Coursera offers individual courses in data-related subjects, such as "The Data Scientist's Toolbox", or "Python Data Structures". You can take these for free, or elect to pay a fee and get an official certificate of completion. Note that individual courses are almost always a part of a larger program called a Specialization, and the cost structure doesn't change much- most learners find themselves just enrolling in the Specialization and taking whichever courses they want.

Specializations: This is Coursera's bread and butter- the specialization. These are groups of ~4-6 courses that are designed to build foundational knowledge in the topic at hand. For example, one of Coursera's most popular Specializations is, "Applied Data Science with Python", offered by the University of Michigan. This particular program has four courses, and starts with the basics of Python programming and data manipulation, and gradually works you up to Machine Learning and Text Mining in later courses.

Specializations are roughly the equivalent of Professional Certificates from edX, and similar to Nanodegrees from Udacity (although the total courseload may be different). Learners and job seekers love Coursera's specializations in part because they do a nice job at being detailed and specific enough to be useful, but broad enough to provide good fundamental knowledge in Data Science, Analytics, or Engineering.

Thoughts from a Data Professional

"I had done some data work before- Excel, super basic SQL, and even taught myself some Python. I tried some sites like Codecademy and DataQuest to try to get the skills to become a Data Scientist, but neither really gave me the foundational knowledge I knew I needed. I signed up for Coursera and realized I love the part-lecture, part-interactive format of the specializations. It took a lot of work and personal drive to not only complete the courses, but actually learn the material, but it was worth it in the end- I finished my specialization in Data Science and eventually landed a job as a Data Scientist at my dream tech company in San Francisco."

Bachelor's & Master's Degrees: Coursera has helped build some highly-rated degree offerings, including both Master's and Bachelor's degrees. At the time of this writing the only data-specific degrees are Master's, while the more technical Bachelor's degrees are in Computer Science, but it's worth noting as you scope out options in the future.

There are only a few Master's degree options, but Coursera is expanding continuously and is looking to add more options. As we mentioned before, Master's Degrees are probably seen as the most legitimate online learning, but also take more time and require a larger financial investment. Also, as of now, Master's Degrees on Coursera are more expensive than those offered by edX, but we'll look more closely at this in the Cost section.

MasterTrack: Somewhat newer in the Coursera portfolio of options is the MasterTrack, which is similar to what we saw from edX in that you can take groups of courses from a particular institution, and if you later decide to enroll in their Master's program you will be able to apply that work to your degree. As of this writing there are only four MasterTrack programs, and neither of the two data-oriented programs are currently active (although it seems they'll be active soon).

One important thing to note as you review your options on Coursera: read the fine print and don't any assumptions about coursework applying to degrees. MasterTrack programs are intended to help you make progress toward an advanced degree, but currently Specializations do not contribute to a Master's (or Bachelor's). For example, Coursera offers a Master's in Applied Data Science through the University of Michigan, and there is also a Specialization in Applied Data Science through the University of Michigan. Although some of the coursework is likely to be similar, coursework in the Specialization would not apply to the degree. That said, it would definitely help you to understand the material and succeed, and it's likely they would take your completion of the Specialization into account when reviewing your application to the Master's program.

Credential

This section will be pretty simple, as the credentialing process is similar to what we saw in the edX portion of this chapter. Let's take a look at each program offering and compare:

Individual Courses: Should you choose to sign up for a paid Coursera subscription, you'll receive an official certificate of completion upon finishing a course. The interesting thing here is that, in order to take an individual course, you usually have to sign up for the Specialization the course is a part of. From there you're free to bounce around and take whichever courses you choose, and it won't affect how much you ultimately pay.

Specializations: Subscribing to Coursera comes with the obvious benefit of receiving a verifiable certificate of completion for the Specialization- for example, the "Specialization in Applied Data Science" from the University of Michigan. As you can imagine, the certificate itself is co-branded with both Coursera and the sponsoring institution:

One of our student's Specialization Certificate (she got a great job as a Data Scientist)

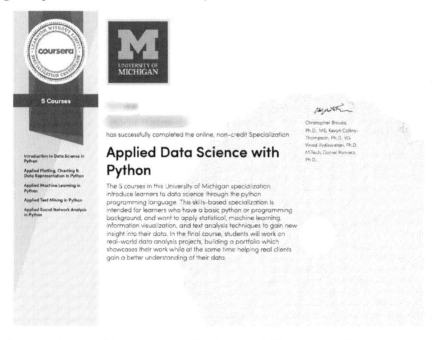

has successfully completed the online, non-credit Specialization

Applied Data Science with Python

The 5 courses in this University of Michigan specialization introduce learners to data science through the python programming language. This skills-based specialization is intended for learners who have a basic python or programming background, and want to apply statistical, machine learning, information visualization, and text analysis techniques to gain new insight into their data. In the final course, students will work on real-world data analysis projects, building a portfolio which showcases their work while at the same time helping real clients gain a better understanding of their data.

One unique thing to note is that, while you will receive a certificate of completion for the whole Specialization, you'll also receive certificates for each individual course along the way. Does this matter? Probably not for most people, but in the event your studies get interrupted it may be nice to have certificates for the courses your were able to complete.

Bachelor's & Master's Degrees: No surprise here- a degree is a degree. Any degree you complete from Coursera will be the same as a degree you complete on campus, be it from the University of Michigan or the Imperial College of London. These are true degrees and carry weight in the job market, but come only through a hefty investment of both time and money.

Those interested in pursuing an advanced degree should take time to weigh the pros and cons wisely, and it is probably beneficial to audit a Specialization through the same institution to see if the coursework interests you enough to spend 1-3 years studying it in a degree program, as well as if you like the format of online learning. Also, some learners consider getting a Bachelor's in a technical field, rather than pursuing a Master's. If you don't currently have a Bachelor's this is probably a good idea, considering that most data roles require a Bachelor's at a minimum (at least in prominent tech companies), but think twice if you've already got a Bachelor's. A Bachelor's degree in a seemingly irrelevant field (such as Communications) combined with a Master's in a technical field (like Data Science) will be more impactful than two Bachelor's degrees (one technical and one non-technical).

Also, if you're serious about pursuing another degree, it will be worth it to push yourself and take more rigorous coursework that goes along with post-graduate education.

Lastly, it's likely that a Master's degree will actually take you less time than starting new Bachelor's program.

MasterTrack: Similarly to the MicroMasters from edX, this certificate carries a little extra weight simply because of the word, "Master's" in the description. Hiring teams will be at least a little more confident in your education background if they know your coursework was at the postgraduate level. Since there are no currently available offerings we won't be able to provide much detail, but go ahead and check in on the MasterTrack programs periodically and see if anything matches what you're looking for.

Cost

All-in costs with Coursera can vary greatly in both total amount and relative to other platforms, and we'll get into specifics here. One aspect worth mentioning up front is that the vast majority of content on Coursera can be accessed for free, and you can get the official certificate with a paid subscription. Coursera has (arguably) the most simple and easy-to-understand pricing of any of the platforms, and many feel it is the best value for the money. Let's dive in.

Individual Courses & Specializations: Since most individual courses are a part of a Specialization, the costs fall in line with each other. Whether you want to take a full Specialization program or just a single course, you'll have to enroll in the full Specialization and sign up for a monthly subscription, most of which are currently $49 per month (although they range from $40-$80 per monthly). Coursera offers a 7-day trial period before you're billed, and if you look around online you may be able to find some coupon codes that give you a discount or a longer unpaid period.

The great part about monthly subscriptions is that you only pay for as much time as it takes to complete the coursework. For example, the Specialization in Applied Data Science from the University of Michigan is estimated to take about 5 months to complete, which would be roughly $250 total. However, if you really want to put a ton of time into it every week and blitz through the material, you could knock it out in a month or two, taking your total cost for the specialization down to about $100. Not bad.

If you've invested in these chapters and are devoting time to learning the information we're teaching you, you're one of the few people who are motivated to break into the field of data and is willing to take action. Those who are motivated to put the work in love Coursera's subscription model because it motivates them to stay on top of their coursework and finish quickly, while still gaining mastery of the principles of successful data work. Compared to Udacity's $399 per month offer, Coursera's $49 per month subscription to be taught by top institutions is tough to beat.

Bachelor's & Master's Degrees: While degrees from Coursera are very valuable and fulfilling experiences, the pricing tends to be less competitive with other platforms offering degrees. The online Master's of Computer Science in Data Science from the University of Illinois will cost you around $22,000 for the whole program, while the Master's in Applied Data Science from the University of Michigan will cost an estimated $32,000-

$42,000 as of the time of this writing. That's not exactly chump change. That said, these are top-tier universities, which is why they're able to command a higher tuition than other institutions.

MasterTrack: These small batches of post-graduate coursework are certainly less expensive than a full Master's, but are also above and beyond what you'd pay for a Specialization from Coursera. We don't have concrete information on what the costs will look like for data-oriented MasterTracks yet, but expect to pay somewhere in the neighborhood of $3,000-$5,000.

That's it. Two of Coursera's main strengths are its partnerships with top institutions and its highly-favored pricing model that incentivizes and rewards those who are willing to devote a concentrated effort to finishing courses or Specializations. Not to mention, even if you take the full estimated time to complete a Specialization, you'd be paying less than you would for similar certificates on other platforms.

Stepping Back

Hopefully the above has been helpful for you to understand the different online learning options in-depth, as well as the costs associated and various credentials available. Remember that, as we said in the beginning, we assumed that you've gone through "Self-Taught vs. Online: The Ultimate Guide" in order to figure out if online learning is right for you. If it is, this chapter on the top 3 online platforms will be a great resource in choosing the right online platform. In this section we're going to take a step back and look at the whole picture of what you're trying to accomplish, and ideally you'll be able to draw some conclusions that make sense of what can feel like a maze of really good options.

What is our outcome?

Your individual outcome is something juicy and personally motivating, like the example in the first section of this chapter: "My outcome is to create and cultivate top-level skills that help me get a fantastic job as a Data Scientist at a great company where I'd be excited to come into work every day". Overall we can say that our outcome is to get you a great job in the field of data. What defines "great" is up to you, but typically people talk about doing interesting work, working at a great company, and getting much better pay as reasons they want to break into this field. Whatever your reasons, make sure they're good ones and know that it is absolutely possible to make the leap if you're willing to put together a strategy (we'll help with that), invest in yourself (like you're doing with this chapter), and do the work.

Since we know our outcome, we need to think about things we can do to contribute to that outcome. We won't cover every detail here, but instead we'll focus on the parts that relate to online learning. Feel free to make a list of your own, but here's a start:

- Build skills relevant to the role you're interested in

- Learn concepts well enough to use on the job and to be successful

- Practice and be able to speak to the concepts or perform well in a whiteboard interview

It may sound overly simplistic, but the reason we're bringing this up is to reinforce the purpose of online coursework- to teach you the skills to get you where you want to be. Unfortunately many people start an online course, do a halfway decent job, and then stick it on their resume, which was the only reason they took the course in the first place. Online courses should be on your resume, but that's not the reason you're taking them.

So, why did we go through sections on credentialing for each platform in this chapter? While having the stamp on your resume is not the main focus, it is a fact that recruiters and hiring managers see that as a signal that you have the skills. If someone sees that you took graduate-level coursework in Data Science & Machine Learning from Harvard, it will have a bigger impact on their perception of you than if you put, "Self-Taught in Data Science and Machine Learning" on your resume- even if you have the same exact knowledge.

With this chapter we want to prepare you for two things: to have the skills necessary to get a job offer and succeed in the role, and to help you get a signal on your resume that will help you get an interview in the first place. The signal is important. It's very true that just because someone took some online courses, or even has a full Master's, from a place like Stanford doesn't mean they're inherently better than a candidate without those credentials. But it's also true that recruiters and hiring managers look for signals like these to determine someone who is more likely to ultimately be a good fit for the role. This is why we've been nudging you in the direction of taking full online programs, particularly those sponsored by a brand-name institution.

We want to cover one more thing, and it may just save you a lot of money. Know this: you don't have to pay for a "Verified" certificate to put the coursework on your resume, and it may not actually matter whether or the program you completed could be verified. Remember that edX and Coursera both have options where you can take full programs for free, and only have to pay if you want a verified certificate.

In all likelihood, you won't need a verified certificate, and it's doubtful that many employers will ask or want to check. You could simply do the entire program and be honest about completing the assignments and checking your work, put the program on your resume, and on the rare chance the employer asks or wants to verify, you can just say, "Truthfully, I did the entire program and completed all the assignments, but I just decided not to pay for the certificate because I was mostly interested in learning the material and getting really good at the concepts. I'm happy to demonstrate any data concepts and undergo some additional technical interviews if you'd like".

What can they say to that? They'll probably say, "No, that's OK", or "Sure, let's do a few more coding challenges". If they say, "No, we don't believe you", then it's probably not a place you want to work anyway.

Do whatever makes you most comfortable. Some people like to go ahead and pay for the certificate because it makes them more motivated, while many just take the courses and add the program to your resume. As long as you're honest and don't say anything that's not true (eg. you have a Master's when you don't, etc.), you'll be fine.

Thoughts from a Hiring Manager

"Yes, we look at credentials. It's a little silly because I know and believe that people who went to brand-name schools aren't necessarily smarter or better at their jobs, but sometimes filtering resumes on those things helps our overall success rate. I like to see candidates that have done some additional coursework in Data Science, because it shows me that they're willing to put in the work.

I wouldn't go through any formal verification for online programs or certificates, but maybe that's just me. I definitely test all candidates for their skills in key concepts, and regardless of degrees or certificates I make sure they can display the knowledge needed to succeed in the role. I am also wary of people who exaggerate their abilities significantly. Everyone does this to an extent, but if you tell me that you're an "Expert" in Python and you can't write a simple loop, it's hard for me to see you as a legitimate candidate."

That's about it for this chapter. Right now is an incredibly exciting time to get into the field of data because there are so many resources online, and much of it is available for free (or inexpensive). You can literally build a brand new, exciting career completely online. Remember that there are a lot of good options, and you don't have to choose the "perfect" one. Realistically, if you're willing to put in the effort, any of the above platforms (as well as many others) will get you in a place to earn a fantastic new role you'll love. The key is you and the effort you put in- many different approaches will work if you will.

6 Figures in 60 Days

Welcome to the most-requested section of the entire guide. We have lots of great chapters available, such as, "Discover Your Path in Data" and "Top Questions from Real Interviews", but this is where the rubber meets the road. This is where you'll get the tools and strategy to get your dream job. This is where you'll win big.

Keep this in mind: while this is the most sought-after strategy we share, it's also the one that requires the most work from you. Getting a good job of any kind is difficult, and often data-related careers are the most competitive roles out there- what that means is that you're going to have to put in the time and effort to see yourself through to success. We're going to give you the strategy and tools you need, but we can't make you put in the work. As Jim Rohn once said, "You can't hire someone else to do your pushups for you".

Before we begin, I want to let you know that you're already succeeding. Most of the developed world looks like this: go to school, get a job you don't really like, put in an average amount of effort, maybe get a 1% raise per year (if you're lucky), and focus on your favorite television shows. That's perfectly fine for some people, but you're one of the few individuals that actually strives to better themselves. You're one of the few people that will invest both time and money into a strategy like this, and you're actually going to take action. This is a big deal, and you should be proud of yourself. My hat's off to you.

I also want to share that I think we're kindred souls. Both I and everyone else at Learn-Data was once in a situation you may be familiar with: in a job you don't like, with a little-known college brand, and no big successes in the family to learn from. We've also had to make our own way in this world. We know what it's like to stay up late working, only to get up at 4am the next morning and get back to work on the dream. We know what it's like to sacrifice free time for the dream.

Let's get down to the nitty-gritty. As I mentioned, this will work if you do. Don't start unless you're committed to seeing this through, because there will probably be times in your job search when you'll want to give up. Get committed.

We're also going to assume that you're at least somewhat qualified for a role in data. You've probably done an online course or two, or may even have a background in something quantitative. You don't have to have a long history in Data Science or Data Analytics or anything else, but if you're brand-spanking new and have never opened Excel or have no idea what SQL is, this may not be the section for you. In this case we suggest starting with the section, "Finding Your Path in Data", and then move on to "Self Taught vs. Online Courses: The Ultimate Guide". From there, we recommend getting to work teaching yourself core concepts or enrolling in an online class. You do need to have the ability to perform well in a data-driven role, and we don't want to assume that any employer is willing to train you up from zero.

That said, let's get down to business. This is going to be a fantastic section, and both your financial and time commitment will pay off exponentially. Our outcome here is to help you get a great job in data- it could be a Data Analyst, Data Scientist, Data Engineer, or any other subtypes within these roles. The structure of this section is an 8 week strategy, but keep in mind that your mileage may vary. Some people take longer to find a job, others do so much quicker. We recommend reading this section all the way through first, then going back and taking it week-by-week. That way, if you start moving quickly and have an onsite interview in week two, for example, you'll know exactly where to find the onsite preparation info in this chapter.

Are you ready? Let's do it.

One of the main themes in this chapter is going to be outreach, which to us means reaching out to connections and applying to jobs. This is a crucial part of the process, and we're going to be a little more strategic than most people are. Most potential candidates use the "spray & pray" technique: they just blast their resume out to a few role postings and then hope and pray they get an interview. Instead, we're going to be smart in our approach.

Keep this in mind: you want to keep generating opportunities, even when you get interviews. One of the biggest mistakes people make is that they stop applying for job once they've got an interview with the hiring manager or an onsite. Don't do this! You want to continue applying to jobs until the moment you've signed an offer letter. This will give you options and help free your mind from any nervousness or anxiety.

The first step: make a list of companies and roles. Use Google Sheets or something similar to create a home base listing companies, their industry, links to the role you're interested in, and fields for things like the date you applied, whether or not you were rejected, etc. This is where you're going to track everything.

Company	Industry	Personal Rank	Employee Count	Role Link 1	Role Link 2	Connection	Notes	Applied Date	Status

Ready for something outside the norm? One of our key strategies is to start applying and interviewing at the companies you're least excited about. It may sound counterintuitive, but there is great power in this. The best way to do this is to rank every company on your list from most ideal to least (1 through 100, or through however many you have), and then start applying from the **bottom** of your list.

Why do this? Wouldn't it make more sense to concentrate our efforts on the most interesting and exciting opportunities? Actually, no, and here's why: you need to practice interviewing. Let me repeat that: you need practice. It doesn't matter if you have a PhD or can write amazing machine learning code- you're going to need to get some reps under your belt in order to eventually succeed and get an offer.

This is a secret to applying to jobs that the vast majority of people don't get. Here's what most people do: they find a few jobs they'd love ("dream jobs"), get really excited, work their butt off to get an interview, and then totally mess up when they get the chance to speak with someone. They miss their opportunity at their dream role, not because they're unqualified, but because they haven't taken the time to cultivate the skill of interviewing.

If you've done this before, don't worry- everyone has. Now you know better. Now you have a strategy in play that will allow you to get exposure to multiple opportunities, sharpen your skills, and eventually get your ideal role at a fantastic company. That sounds a lot better than going for your dream role right away and blowing it.

Here's another thing you may not have thought of: go ahead and apply to roles even if you're not 100% confident you would take the role. Going through these low-risk opportunities will be a great way to sharpen your interviewing skills and get to a place where you can really perform when it's for a role you're very serious about.

"But won't I be wasting other people's time?"

Because you're a polite person, you may be concerned that applying for a job you don't really want will be dishonest or a waste of the company's time. It's good to be empathetic in this way, and you don't want to apply to jobs that you'd never take, but think about it this way- for a given role, even if you're not super interested, is there anything that would make you take the job? What if they offered you a salary of $200,000/yr? What if the manager was your ideal leader? What if the company was experiencing incredible growth and there was a clear path to a leadership role in a year or two?

Another main theme is practice. Once you do get interviews, you're going to need to take time to rehearse your answers to questions- not just writing them, but saying them out loud. This will help you become confident and ready to succeed in the interviews. You need to approach interviewing in the same way you'd approach learning SQL, Python, or any other technical skill- as a skill unto itself. Some people feel that if they have the right technical skills and meet the job requirements, they'll get the job once they get an interview. They often don't. When they don't, they usually do one of two things: blame the company or process, saying things like, "I guess they just wanted someone who went to Harvard" (or something similar), or they feel that their coding or technical skills were the reason they didn't receive the opportunity, so they enroll in another online course, put in the work, and get the credential- only to find themselves in the same position later.

Let's be clear: the opportunities you receive are a function of your value (ability to do the job, potential, etc.), and your ability to communicate that value. You get what you communicate. Write that down now- you get what you communicate!

Week 1

Alright, week one is where it all gets started. If you haven't made your list of companies yet, go ahead and re-read the section above and create the spreadsheet. This is going to allow you to keep lots of opportunities going at the same time, track your progress, and identify your weak points so you know exactly what to improve.

Once you've got that, it's time to get started. Your first step is to stack-rank your list, with #1 being the job you want most and the last number being the job you're least interested in. When your list is ranked, sort it from high to low- we're going to start with the least-desirable opportunities on your list. Let's review the why behind this one more time: starting with the least-desirable companies will help you get practice without risking losing out on something fantastic. Consider this free 1:1 tutoring in interview skills, or at least as close as you can get without paying someone huge sums of money. Remember, you're not doing anything wrong by taking this approach as long as you're open to the possibility of working with these companies. Who knows? Maybe you'll be surprised by one of these "not-as-good" opportunities and go ahead and take it. Some readers have interviewed at a company they didn't think was very interesting, but found out there was a great growth strategy and they really clicked with the hiring manager- and they ultimately took the job over their "top companies".

Now what? The next step can be somewhat daunting if you don't have much experience: outreach. Outreach, for our purposes, simply means applying to jobs directly (reaching out to the company) or reaching out to connections in your network that may be able to help you get an interview. We're going to go over the latter in detail, but first let's make sure we understand how to apply directly online correctly.

Applying Online

Is it true that all online job postings are simply a, "black hole" for resumes? Not at all. Companies large and small actively review applications that come through online and move candidates to the interview stage if they think there's a potential fit. You're probably going to apply to many jobs through online portals, so there are a few things to keep in mind:

Make sure your resume looks great and speaks to the job you're applying for. For now just make sure it's one page (seriously), highlights your relevant accomplishments, and doesn't have a ton of fluff that is irrelevant to the job. Did you get a silver medal for a marketing competition in college five years ago? Go ahead and leave it out unless you're applying for a marketing role. Last piece of advice: don't obsess over the resume. Find some good examples online, copy them, and move on.

You won't hear back on a lot of applications- don't read into it too much. It's highly unlikely that you're going to get an interview for every application, so when you get a rejection letter (or nothing at all), just keep your head up and keep moving. The other side to this is that if you're submitting a lot of applications (in the ballpark of 20) and you're getting rejected for everything, you may need to re-think the roles you're applying to. Are they entry-level, or do they require a lot of experience you don't have? If you're not getting any interviews at all it may be time to apply to a different type of role, potentially something with slightly lower requirements.

These are the basics of submitting job applications online. Don't expect miracles, but plenty of people get great jobs starting with an online application process. Still, we want to make sure we're being as effective as possible, and applying through a referral is one of the best ways to put yourself in the running for a great job. Let's take a look at how that works.

Our basic process here is that, for companies on our list, we're going to leverage a social network (LinkedIn is the best for this) to find connections that work at the company, or connections of connections that work at the company. One basic way to do this is to just use LinkedIn search tools to look up employees in the company who are a 1st or 2nd connection.

Let's say you found an interesting role at Google. Start by looking for connections you have that work at Google (meaning you and the person are directly connected). If you can find someone, shoot them a message that says something like:

"Hi Sam,

Hope you're doing well. I'm reaching out because I saw an interesting Product Analyst role open at Google that looks like it fits my experience pretty well. Would you be open to submitting a referral for me?

Thanks,

Your Name"

That's it- short and sweet. Don't write a lot and don't complicate it. They don't need to know excessive details about the bootcamp you went to or about how this is your dream job. Write a greeting, tell them why you're reaching out, and ask them one simple yes or no question. Nothing more. It's highly likely that they'll say, "Sure, can you send me your resume and a link to the role?" Then you're set.

You can also do this for 2nd level connections (people who are connected to somebody you're connected to, but not connected directly to you). This will be a little different because you're not going to reach out to the person at the company directly- you're going to reach out to the person you know. Here's what it looks like: let's say you're interested in an Operations Analyst role at Uber. You look through LinkedIn to see if you're connected to anyone at Uber, but no luck. You do see that your friend Tom is connected to someone named Kara who works in recruiting at Uber. Here's what you send:

"Hi Tom,

Hope you're doing well. I'm reaching out because I've been looking into some roles at Uber, and I noticed you're connected to Kara ___. Do you know her well enough to introduce me? (Include a link to the person's profile)

Thanks,

Your Name"

Short and sweet. Sensing a theme here? Give them a greeting, tell them why you're reaching out, and ask a simple yes or no question. If they do connect that person, use the other email template above (mention the exact position) and ask for a referral. This is the formula for successful outreach, and it's not complicated.

To sum it up, our three buckets for outreach are direct applications, reaching out to connections that work at the company, and reaching out to connections who are connected to people that work at the company. Your chances at landing an interview will be better with referrals, but you can still get interviews for great jobs by applying online.

The main thing here is to stay on top of outreach throughout the process and keep lots of opportunities on your plate. One of the biggest mistakes candidates make is spending all their time and effort on one or two companies, then having to start from scratch after a few weeks. We want to have lots of options so we're constantly moving in the right direction.

Lastly, here are a few reminders: make sure you start with the least-desirable companies first. This will enable you to get plenty of practice having conversations, and by the time you get to the big leagues you'll be polished and ready.

You also want to make sure you're taking good notes and tracking your progress. Create a spreadsheet with companies, roles, dates you applied, when the recruiter reached out, and what the status is (applied, rejected, interviewing, offer). On the same spreadsheet, create another tab that will serve as a repository for all the questions you're asked during the process. While you're on the phone with recruiters, make a note of the questions they asked (as long as it doesn't interfere with your concentration). Pro tip: make sure you use pen and paper, rather than typing on the computer- the person on the other end of the phone can hear you typing, and it's annoying and slightly odd.

Whether you take notes during the call or not, do a quick post-mortem after each call. In the spreadsheet, write each question asked, who asked it (e.g. recruiter, hiring manager), what your response was, and what you'd do better next time. As you accumulate questions, you'll start to notice the same questions asked over and over- that means you should spend time writing out your answers and practicing them out loud.

While you're evaluating the call, it's also a good idea to note anything the recruiter mentioned that may be valuable to you later. For example, a recruiter might say, "Yea, believing in our mission is something they look for". Great! Now you know that when you have a call with the hiring manager you'll want to be able to articulate how the company's mission resonates with you personally. The best candidates understand this: recruiters are your friend. They want you to succeed. They are trying to fill roles and their performance is often judged based on how many candidates they bring in that are ultimately hired. It doesn't mean you can be bad or sloppy- it just means that you both want the same thing- to get a great job and be successful.

Week 2

By Week 2, you should have a good groove going. You've probably got a routine of reaching to people or applying to 3-5 jobs per day, and what's important at this point is to stick to it. One way that people go wrong is that they reach out to lots of people, send out lots of applications, and finally start getting interviews, and when they do, they stop applying to jobs. Don't do that! Even as you get interviews, keep reaching out to connections and applying to jobs- you want to have a lot of opportunities on your plate. Keep creating new opportunities for yourself until you have a signed offer, period.

Outreach in this stage shouldn't be any different than last week, so we won't spend a ton of time on it. Hopefully you're getting some recruiter interviews set up, so we're going to focus on doing a great job when you actually get on the phone with someone. The preparation process is fairly straightforward, but there are a few dos and don'ts.

Do:

Understand what the company does at a basic level

Get a list of questions (we have a list in this section)

Physically write your answers down

Practice your answers out loud

Don't:

Look up company-specific questions on Glassdoor or online

Spend a disproportionate amount of time on any one interview

Get too stressed or nervous

When it comes to the questions themselves, candidates often want to dive deep into Glassdoor or scour Google for exact interview questions a particular company will ask. If they're interviewing at Twitter, they want to know what the questions are for Twitter. If they're interviewing at Airbnb, they want to know exactly what Airbnb   asks.
Here's the thing: recruiters almost always ask the same questions, regardless of whether it's a huge tech company or a small startup.

Recruiters want to know:

- About your current role and how well your experience fits the role they have open

- Why you're interested in the company

- Basic items like compensation expectations, verifying you're willing to work where the role is located, etc.

That's mostly it. You might get some questions like, "What tech stack do you use?" or "What's your familiarity with SQL?", but the good news is that you can study and practice the same 10 or so questions for recruiter calls and you'll generally be set for any company you apply to. The main message here is that you shouldn't spend a lot of your time researching specific interview questions for recruiter calls. That time is better spent writing out your answers and practicing saying them out loud. Our other chapter, "Top Questions from Real Interviews", will have specific interview questions, but for now keep these themes in mind.

Lastly, it's natural to feel a little anxious about interviews, but don't get too stressed or nervous. The strategy we're laying out here is exactly what will help curb that anxiety and help you be relaxed and performing really well. You're going to get lots of practice repetitions at the "Tier 2" companies before you go after the big ones. Every time you do an interview, you get more comfortable (so do lots of them). You're also going to be very prepared for the interviews you do have. Writing interview answers down and practicing them out loud will be a tremendous boost to your confidence, which by itself will help you communicate clearly and with passion, and you'll have much more success.

At the end of the day, just enjoy these conversations and learn what you can. You're going to have lots of opportunities in your career, and no one job is going to make or break your life. If you're the type of person who has invested in this program and is willing to put in the effort, things are going to work out well for you over time.

Week 3

Wow, three weeks already- time is probably flying by for you, and that's a good thing. At this point you may be getting interviews with hiring managers. If not, don't worry- just keep doing outreach and use the info in the Week 2 section to do a great job on recruiter calls.

In this section we're going to discuss the hiring manager interview, which usually comes after the recruiter interview, as well as the data challenge. The purpose of the recruiter interview is to make sure you meet the base qualifications for the role, and the hiring manager is going to take that one step further to understand your abilities at a deeper level and get a sense of how you'd fit into the team's mission.

These interviews can vary a bit, but they often involve the hiring manager telling you about the role and team, you explaining your experience, and a case question. A "case" question is essentially a mock scenario that is a good example of what the role will entail. Here's an example question that a company like Uber might ask:

"Let's say that the number of new drivers goes down. How would you dig into that metric to figure out what the problem is?"

As you can see, it's more about getting an idea of your thought process than it is determining whether or not you know a specific technical concept.

These questions are very important. It's often the case that hiring managers want to know that you have a strong problem-solving ability and coherent thought process more than they want someone to have experience in some particular statistical theory or something of that nature. This is your chance to shine and show that you're a logical and creative thinker that can solve problems effectively.

How do you find and practice these problems? This is the time to look up questions specific to the company. If you're interviewing for a Data Scientist role at Uber, start Googling Data Scientist interview questions at Uber. For the big companies you should be able to find some good information, but if you're interviewing at a smaller company or just aren't finding questions, try looking up a competitor or getting more general in your search. "Data Analyst Interview Questions" or "Data Scientist Interview Questions" should have some good results.

One more thing to keep in mind: make sure that you're writing down the questions you're asked as much as you can, as well as your answers. At the end of the week, evaluate yourself and write out how you could have answered the question better. Over time this information will be a treasure-trove of valuable insight into the typical questions for the role you're targeting. Also be sure to keep your tracker up to date (applied, interviewing, rejected, etc.). The tracker should be completed in such a way that anyone can glance at it and within 60 seconds understand what you've done and where you are in your job search.

Now, let's discuss the infamous data challenge.

If you've made it this far, you're doing incredibly well-congratulations! The data challenge is a way for a company to understand your ability to think through problems and present analyses in a compelling way. These are typically larger, multi-part prompts that ask you to analyze a data set, dig into abnormalities and/or find opportunities, discuss your findings, and recommend action items. They are most common for Analyst and Data Scientist paths, but are possible for other data roles as well.

The first step is that the recruiter will let you know how much time you'll have to complete the data challenge (usually 2-4 days), and will ask when you'd like to receive it. Always schedule it so you'll have a full weekend to work on the project. For example, if the assignment needs to be returned in 48hrs, ask to have it sent early Saturday morning (recruiters can schedule these emails, so they don't have to send it to you manually). You're going to want to give yourself a full two days to work on it if needed.

When the time comes, the recruiter will email you a prompt and a dataset, usually in CSV form, although occasionally a company will you have pull data from a cloud database such as BigQuery. He or she will also remind you of the timeline for delivery. The prompt will have the details of the challenge, and will also say something like, "The estimated time to complete this is 3-5hrs". Ignore this. You should absolutely take as much time as you need. There are no extra points for doing it within the "estimated time", and It's incredibly rare that anyone from the company would ask how long you spent on the data challenge. If they do, just be honest and say you got really interested in the project and time flew by.

Your first priority is to not be overwhelmed, worried, or stressed. When you get the email, don't start reading the prompt until you're actually ready to get started and spend at least an hour working on it. For example, if you're going to grab coffee with a friend Saturday morning, don't read the prompt and then walk out the door to meet up with them. This is for two reasons: 1. Some people get stressed, and it affects their mental state negatively, and 2. Even if you don't get stressed, your brain might start to come up with hypotheses and explanations for whatever problem you're going to work on, without even having looked at the data! You don't want to approach the data with mental biases because they can prevent you from seeing the truth in the data.

When you do settle in to work on it, get excited. This is an excellent way to show your skills, and for most people it's a lot better than an extra 2-3hrs of technical and problem solving in-person interviews. In the comfort of your own home you'll be able to relax and enjoy the process of solving interesting problems with data. One note: a data challenge is almost always reflective of the work you'd be performing on the job, so if for some reason it's something you would never have an interest in doing, you may want to bow out of the process. This is unlikely if you've made it this far, but keep in mind that it will line up pretty closely with your day-to-day.

Once you are settled in, read the prompt fully. One of the biggest mistakes candidates make is that they read the first question and jump right in. DON'T TOUCH THE DATA YET! You need to develop a firm understanding of the entire problem and how the questions are connected before you start writing code. Read the prompt fully.

The next step is to start taking notes. Copy the prompt into a Gdoc or your preferred text editor (or print it out and take notes by hand). At this point you also want to look at the datasets and see what you're working with. You should be able to answer each one of these questions:

What is Question 1 asking me? How would I restate it in my own words? What about Question 2... etc.?

What is the general theme I'm sensing from the questions? What business problem am I solving? Am I digging into a metric anomaly? Am I looking for ways to increase users, revenue, etc.?

What's being asked of me? Am I being asked to come up with new product features? Am I being asked to recommend a strategy? Will I be presenting this to a group in my onsite?

Who is the audience? Am I presenting this to the Head of Data Science, or the Head of Marketing, or both? Hint: most data challenges have an audience of multiple stakeholders, including technical and non-technical.

What's my output? Is it slides? Is it a written document? Is it up to me? Pro tip: if the prompt leaves the presentation medium up to you, use slides (Google Slides is pretty good). Everyone makes fun of PowerPoint and slides in general, but it's a medium that makes it easy to communicate and get your point across, and it's something that most people are used to receiving on a daily basis. Use slides unless the prompt asks you for another format or specifically asks that you not use slides.

Again, don't write one word of code until you're able to answer the above questions. Preparation is crucial in data challenges, and is also one of the things separating really effective people from novices in a real-life work setting.

Your preparation phase should take anywhere from 20 minutes to 1 hour. Creating a plan is going to not only help you execute the task more effectively, but will also give you confidence and help you feel in command of the situation. This is a lot different than what happens to most candidates, which is that they jump in with both feet, start writing lots of code, have to backtrack and effectively waste several hours of time, and ultimately feel stressed, overwhelmed, and desperate. Preparing as prescribed will help you win in the end, so follow this plan and you'll be in great shape.

Once you've got a good idea of what the prompt is asking and what your approach will be, start doing your exploratory data analysis. We won't go into too much detail here because there is a lot of variability depending on the prompt, dataset, and role you're applying for, but use the skills you've developed in your online learning or self-study to work through the challenge effectively. If it's difficult, that's good- it's supposed to be a challenge.

Once you've worked through the problem, developed some hypotheses, and feel like you have a good point of view, you need to create the deliverable. We'll assume you're going to create a short presentation (slides).

First of all, go back and check the prompt to see if they gave you direction on the number of slides, and plan to follow it if so. If they say, "Your presentation should be 8-10 slides", make it 10 slides. Not 11. Most companies will impose a limit on slide count because A. they don't want to spend tons of time reading your presentation, and B., it forces you to be clear and concise with your findings. In the real world you're not going to be able to do 50 slides for a small or medium-sized project because no one would want to sit through that.

The data challenge is great for testing your ability to work through problems and write code, but what most people don't realize is that the company is also testing for your ability to communicate. "Right" or "wrong" isn't as important as your ability to take a vague problem, form logical and coherent ideas based on data, and communicate those ideas.

Just like communication is important in your interviews, it's important here. The people who succeed at the highest level aren't necessarily the greatest technologists in the world (although they can be), but they are the people who can communicate the best. Think about Elon Musk. He is certainly a genius, but is he the most knowledgeable person in the world about electric cars? Nope. Is he the greatest rocket engineer on the planet? Not even close. He succeeds because he does understand things at a technical level, and he's able to articulate a vision that people find compelling. Cheap space travel. Saving the planet by reducing emissions. These are large, audacious goals that anyone can understand and rally behind, and that's why people are willing to not only invest in him, but follow him.

The great news is that this is within your power- you just have to apply yourself. Communicate clearly. Start with a few bullet-point summary of your ideas, and then show the audience how you came to those conclusions. Avoid text-heavy slides and use charts and visuals when you can. Give a simple recommendation or set of recommendations that anyone can interpret easily. If you can, quantify the upside of going forward with your recommendation(s) and acknowledge the downside. Be thoughtful in your approach and you will do well.

That's about it. The data challenge is often a lot of work, but it's also often the most enjoyable part of the process. Many candidates find that they love doing the project and are excited to the same kind of work in the role, which is a fantastic situation to be in.

When it's finally done, save the documents (usually as a PDF) and send to the recruiter. Feel free to add a note letting them know you enjoyed working on the project (you can even say it was, "fun"). Then you can relax and move on to other things. Expect to wait up to a week to hear back, and it's probably OK to follow-up at around the 3-day mark unless the recruiter said it would take longer.

Week 4

Alright, so now you've been searching for jobs for one month. If you don't have an offer by now, don't worry- it's perfectly normal. It can take several weeks to several months to get an offer for a role, depending on your level of outreach, what roles you're going for, the time of year, and the job market where you live.

Realistically it doesn't matter how long it takes, does it? If you had a baby, how long would you give him to walk before you said, "OK, that's enough. I guess you're not going to walk." Every parent in the world would have their child keep trying until they figured it out- that's why most people in the world walk.

You need a similar mentality in your job search, but we'll refine it a little bit. If this is something you really want to do, you're going to keep trying until you get the result you're after. Our key to success is that we're going to be constantly improving and learning from every mistake and failure. Every time you have an interview, you're going to get better. Every time you do a data challenge, you're going to get better. Every single time.

A few strategic notes: as always, keep track of questions and do weekly post-mortems on what you can improve. Getting a job is a skill, and you need to constantly improve that skill. Secondly, don't be afraid to change course a little bit. One thing I see with some candidates is that they aim super high and lose sight of what's realistic for them at this point in their career. For example, if you took a 6-week course in data science and have a Bachelor's degree in communications, it's not likely you're going to get an offer for Senior Machine Learning Engineer role at Google right now. To be clear, you can have anything you want over time, provided you put in the work and develop yourself. Just know that for certain positions it may take some time to build up to be ready to enter that role.

Another example: let's say you want to be a Data Scientist, but after 50 applications you haven't had one hiring manager interview. You could keep trying, or you could explore Data Analyst roles at companies that have a strong Data Science team. While being a Data Analyst isn't your ultimate outcome, it could be a great way to get your foot in the door at a great company. From there you can prove yourself and eventually work your way into a Data Scientist role. Know this: for people with non-traditional backgrounds, it is much easier to move to a more advanced position within a company (by doing great work, building relationships, etc.) than it is to get an advanced position at a brand new company. Assuming you have good relationships and do great work, your current company is much more likely to take a chance on you than an outside company will be. The moral of the story is: aim high, but don't be afraid to adjust along the way and consider potential "stepping-stone" jobs that will help you reach your ultimate destination.

Week 5-7

Somewhere in weeks 5-7 you'll probably have onsite interviews. If this hasn't happened for you yet, don't worry- just stay on top of the process outlined in early weeks: maintain a good level of outreach, focus on the right things at the right time, and learn from every interaction/interview you have. Keep going and eventually you will get where you want to go.

One small note- if you've been actively reaching out about 10-20 jobs per week for five weeks, and haven't made it to the hiring manager interview yet, it may be time to step back and think about how "near-term realistic" you're being. As we said in the previous section, you can eventually do any role you want, no matter how sophisticated it sounds. You could even be a brain surgeon if you wanted to. That said, things don't always work with the timeline you have in mind. To be as extreme as possible and continue with the brain surgeon analogy: yes, you can definitely become a brain surgeon, but you won't become one with just a bachelor's degree, no matter how interested and passionate you are. You'd need to go through the process of getting your doctorate, doing a medical residency, etc., and then you'd get to operate on people's brains.

Thankfully no job in data is like brain surgery, and the vast majority aren't life and death. The education requirements that are a big barrier in fields such as medicine aren't as much as a barrier for us. What is important, however, is experience. Even roles that say they require a Master's or PhD in the job description will have exceptions for people who have "equivalent practical experience", which is great for those that are self-taught.

What we're driving at here is that there is a certain point in which it may make sense to temporarily lower your sights in order to eventually get your dream job, or what you think is your dream job. As we said in the previous section, there are a lot of great "stepping stone" jobs, such as a Data Analyst, that can lead to some of the more desired roles such as Data Scientist or Data Engineer. Be smart and think about how to best get to your ultimate outcome strategically, rather than getting fixated on one specific job title.

Let's get back to the meat of this chapter: onsite interviews. These are the most exciting part of the job hunt, but also the most daunting. First of all, if you've got an onsite interview, you should absolutely be happy and proud of yourself for getting this far. Onsites can range from a few hours to a full day, and no company would ever waste this time on someone who couldn't do the role- this means that when a company brings you onsite they are serious about hiring you. Congratulations!

The work isn't over yet, though. For a single role, companies are probably bringing 3-6 candidates in to the office for interviews, and you have to be the best one.

The good news is that you can practice hard and smart, and take advantage of all the controllables to give yourself a great chance of succeeding. Let's get started.

The process will start with scheduling, and once the date is confirmed the recruiter will give you a list of people you'll be interviewing with. Pay attention to this, because we're going to do research on these people later. Some companies will also tell you what type of interview each person (or group of people) will be conducting: technical, culture fit, business case, etc. That is very valuable information to understand.

Our first step is to look back at the role posting (you kept the link in your doc, right?). Create a doc in Google Docs or wherever you take notes, and start by pasting in the job description and requirements. Now, you're going to go through the job description line-by-line, picking out pieces of information and taking notes on the work you've done that is applicable to the specific point. For example, let's say you're interviewing for a Data Scientist role, and one of the bullet points in the job description is this:

"Utilize statistical or machine learning techniques to assess marketing efficiency and recommend optimal spend by channel and by product"

Underneath that line in your doc, write down anything and everything you can think of that relates to this, even if it was just a project you did in your spare time. If there's a bullet point where you literally have no experience, just make a note and move on to the next item (we'll circle back to that later).

This is an extremely important step, so don't skip it! Hiring managers/companies aren't just interested in your skills- they're interested in your applicable skills. Throughout the interview process they'll be asking themselves, "Will this person be happy and successful in this role specifically?". By understanding this and implementing this strategy you're able to give yourself a leg up on the competition. You want to brainstorm all the work you've done related to the exact job you're interviewing for, and tailor your communication to speak to that specifically.

Here's one way that people trip themselves up: they emphasize the "cool" projects they've done, or work that they find interesting, rather than focusing on what the hiring manager is interested in (which you know from the job description). Neural nets are really cool, but if it's not a part of the job description and wouldn't realistically come in to play in the role, don't bring it up! It sounds very counterintuitive, but companies are more interested in finding a great fit for the exact position than they are interested in someone who's done a lot of cool projects.

As you can see, it is crucial that you fit in to what the hiring manager is looking for specifically. It's good to let yourself shine- just know that their main concern is bringing on someone who will be happy and successful in the role, rather than someone who is good at lots of different things and may be more interested in different types of work.

Our next step is research. We can chunk this into a few categories: research on the company itself, research on the people you're interviewing with, and research on the questions you'll be asked. With those in mind, let's dive in.

First, you want to start digging into the company itself, starting with some high-level information: What do they do? How do they monetize their business? In what ways are they expanding? We can use a company like Lyft to illustrate. If you've got an onsite with Lyft you definitely know that their in the ride-hailing business and compete with Uber. What else could you find if you started digging in? You might use Google or ask around and find out that they're interested in expanding the business-to-business part of their revenue, which could potentially be selling Lyft credit packages to companies as a perk for their employees. You may also come across info that you didn't realize: for example, did you know that (as of the time of this writing), Lyft operates predominantly in the US, with just a little penetration in Canada but no where else in the world? Unless you found that information out, you might have guessed that such a big company offered their service all over the world, particularly since their main competitor (Uber) operates in lots of international markets.

You could use that information in a few different ways. First of all, being informed about the business helps you know what not to bring up. In the case of Lyft, when you're asked about what you're looking for in your next role, you'll want to leave out anything like, "Working for a company with a big international reach". It sounds obvious, but you'd be surprised what candidates say in interviews!

You can also use the information to craft your own thought-provoking questions. For example, in your Lyft interview you might ask, "What does international expansion look like for Lyft over the next 3-5 years?" This is a great question because you get to learn about the strategic direction of the company and position yourself as someone who's interested in the long-term vision.

Make sure that you devote a good amount of time to researching the company, how they operate, how they're expanding, and their values. It is very important to get an understanding of the company's values and think about how you relate to them. For example, one of Google's core values is: "Focus on the user and all else will follow". Prior to the interview you'd want to think about this and the other values, and think about your viewpoint. In this case, when have you "focused on the user"? Why do you think that is important? Having a great understanding of the company's values will help you succeed in the interview. In fact, many companies have a "culture interview" as a part of the onsite process to make sure that whichever candidate they hire will fit in with the values of the company.

Our main strategy during the research phase is to look up themes and ideas, and start making lists of potential questions. You should also leverage sites like Glassdoor and Blind, as well as general Google searching, to find actual questions asked in interviews. Amass a list of questions, then trim the list by combining questions that are roughly the same. For example, if you have one question that asks you to dig into a decline in a delivery orders metric, and another that asks you to investigate a large spike in new user traffic, you can safely combine them because the general methodology will be the same.

The point here isn't to memorize answers to specific questions- it's to gain an understanding of the types of questions you're likely to be asked and then create a framework for answering them effectively. Your total list of questions, including technical questions, shouldn't be longer than 20-30 questions.

Next step: write answers down and practice saying them out loud. This is one of the most valuable things you'll do in your job search. Make sure that your answers are clear, concise, and correct. Make sure they address the question without being too wordy. Do research and see if you can find other perspectives on the same questions. Being thoughtful and putting in the effort at this stage will help increase your chances of success in the interview and will keep you on the path to getting your dream job.

Once you've got your confidence up for the interview, it's time to research your interviewers. The recruiter should let you know ahead of time whom you'll be interviewing with, so grab that list and start looking people up on LinkedIn (if the recruiter hasn't sent you that list, go ahead and ask). You don't have to go crazy and memorize the interviewers' life stories, and it's probably a bit too much to look them up on Facebook or Instagram. At this point, our goal is to find out a little bit about the interviewers' backgrounds, but more importantly we want to understand what roles they're in so we can better anticipate the type of conversation we'll be having.

Here's some basic info on what various roles might be interested in knowing when you interview with them, but keep in mind that these are just some patterns we've seen in candidate interviews, and not necessarily set in stone. The hiring manager will typically want to know how you'll fit into the team, and may ask case-type questions to get a sense of your problem-solving ability. Candidates often say that these interviews aren't the most difficult ones and tend to be more casual and conversational. Some hiring managers will even say something like, "I'm glad you're here and I'm excited for you to meet everyone. I don't have a lot of questions planned but I'd love to chat and answer any questions you have." All of that said, make sure you bring your A-game. Hiring decisions don't come down to a vote- the hiring manager will be the one who ultimately decides to extend an offer or not. Smile, be friendly, and be prepared to answer case questions as well as questions about why you're interested in joining, what you think about the industry the company is in, etc. If you're interviewing at Apple, talk about how the mission resonates with you and how you're excited about the future of the company. The hiring manager wants to know that you're a great fit and you'll be excited to work at the company.

In addition to the hiring manager, data role onsites often have you meet with a current member of the team or someone who would essentially be a peer of yours. Usually these interviews are going to focus on your technical skills, potentially some case-style questions, and your ability to collaborate effectively. Teammates and peers want to know that you can do the job you're interviewing for, so make sure to brush up on your technical skills and your ability to work through case questions. One note- the recruiter will almost always let you know which interview is the technical interview, but they probably won't have any information about what exactly will be covered. Go back to the job description and read it carefully- what technical skills do they mention? For most data-oriented jobs, SQL is a must, and Python is a big plus (sometimes required for more advanced roles). Also, make sure to give your resume a once-over and be prepared to answer questions based on anything you've listed (anything on your resume is fair game). SQL and Python are typical, but some interviewers will even pull out Tableau if you've got it on your resume- don't be the person that can't do what they said on their resume.

It's highly likely you'll also have interviews with people on other teams, often in non-coding roles. This could be roles like "Business Operations Manager", "Customer Success Manager", or "Product Manager". Often this interviewer is someone that you'd collaborate with on a regular basis (think of them as an internal client or business partner). They're generally going to look at your problem-solving ability (case questions) and your mindset around working cross-functionally (ie., with people in roles outside your team). These are important to do well because your manager and the company needs to understand that people will enjoy working with you and it will be a productive experience for everyone. You probably won't get technical questions here (but it's possible), so focus on answering business problems as well as questions that focus on your ability to work with others. One possible question might be, "Tell me about a time you had to explain something technical to a non-technical person". For more examples, go ahead and search "Cross-functional interviews" online and see what you can dig up.

You may also meet with someone higher up, such as your boss's boss. This could be someone with a title anywhere from "Manager" to "Head of XYZ" to "Director" or "VP". These interviews may seem intimidating, but you shouldn't stress. The higher-up wants to know that you'll be a good fit for the team and have potential to grow and develop. They're also looking for any red flags that might pop up, such as "not being a team player". These are important and you should practice, but work on making a good impression and articulating your interest in the company and you should be good to go. As always, be prepared for business case questions and "Tell me about a time…" questions in case they come up.

The last type of interview we'll discuss is the culture interview. This is usually with someone who is at a similar level but on a different team, or it could be one of your teammates. That said, it could be anyone of any level, and it's often a wise choice to think of every interview as a culture interview.

Anyone in the interview roster may ask you questions about the company's mission, why you're interested, how you are to collaborate with, etc., because everyone wants to know that they're going to enjoy having you on the team. The good news is that the culture component of the interview process should be a place for you to shine. Write out the mission and think about how it resonates with you. Do your research and think about questions that might come up. Come up with a great answer for, "Why are you interested in this role?", and "Why do you want to work at ABC, Inc.?". Plenty of candidates will have the technical chops and problem-solving skills, and so will you- if it comes down to the culture fit, make sure you leave no stone unturned and have great answers.

These interviews go a lot further than questions about why you want to work at the company, or how you feel about their mission. Companies want to understand how you learn and how you approach your work. Here are some other questions you may be asked:

- Tell me about a time you failed

- Tell me about a time you had to give feedback to a teammate or coworker

- Tell me about a time when you taught yourself something new

In one sense, the culture interviews are easy because you're not being tested on a specific subject or being asked to whiteboard code, but in some ways they are more difficult. It's tough to prepare specific answers for all the possible questions, especially since you'll be asked to provide examples of specific situations that relate to the topic at hand. That said, you plan is simple:

research questions ahead of time, go through the process of writing out questions and saying them out loud, and take your time when you're in the interview. When the interviewer asks you a question, it's OK to pause for a few moments and think of a good example. They understand that these questions aren't the easiest to answer, so feel free to take a little time to come up with something.

The key points to illustrate here are that you align with their culture, you're collaborative and good to work with, you have empathy for others, and you're reflective enough to learn from your mistakes. That's the kind of person companies want to hire, and if you put the work in you'll be able to stand out from the crowd.

The last thing we're going to cover in this section is what to do after the onsite interview. This is important, and unfortunately most candidates do great prep work before an interview, do a great job in the interview, but neglect to do a few simple, key things that can make a difference in their ultimate success.

First of all, the recruiter will often want to round up with you after all the interviews (in-person or over the phone). Their purpose is to check in, get your thoughts, and let you know they'll be following up. This is your opportunity to be nice and friendly, and express gratitude for all the work they've done. Thank them for organizing everything. Let the recruiter know you enjoyed chatting with everyone and had a great experience. You can also tee up the follow-up emails (more on that in a moment) by letting the recruiter know you'd love to send thank-you notes to the interviewers, and it would be great if he or she could send you the email addresses. Even though you're probably drained from bringing your A game all day, take time to be friendly with the recruiter. This may help you get considered for another opportunity in the future if the one you're on site for doesn't work out.

At the end of the day, send follow-up emails to the interviewers. Let them know you enjoyed chatting with them and learning about the team. Make each message slightly tailored to the person you're sending it to- if you had a great chat about optimizing user wait times for food delivery, go ahead and mention that.

Most candidates fall off here. They think they either did a great job in the interview or didn't, and they'll get the job or they won't. That is partially true. For most jobs in data fields, sending a follow-up note won't be the difference between getting the role or not.

So why send it? Because you want to keep the door open for future opportunities if the current one doesn't work out. You want to be just a little more memorable in some way. Sending a follow-up note can make a difference in you being considered for other roles in the future, so go ahead and thank them for their time.

Our final point applies only if you didn't get an offer. If this hasn't happened to you yet, it will. Even the best and brightest get rejected, so don't take it to heart. You'll have to do a postmortem and reflect on what you could have done better, but there is one action you can do right away: send another follow-up note, this time to just the hiring manager (and potentially their manager if you interviewed with them and had a good rapport). Yes, really.

Here you're going to thank the hiring manager again, and let them know that although you're disappointed in the outcome, you enjoyed meeting and think it's "definitely the type of team you'd like to be a part of some day". Close the short email with, "Thanks again, and please don't hesitate to let me know if there are other opportunities in the future". Believe it or not, this tiny email can get you a job.

Thoughts from a Data Candidate

"I rejected at my dream company (for my dream role) twice. The 2nd time, I sent a nice follow-up email to the hiring manager and let him know I enjoyed meeting his team and would love to hear about future opportunities. He got back to me a week later and offered me a role on his team- turns out he got approval from his boss to hire one more person, and he chose me. I still had to do great in the interview, but I do think the follow-up note made a difference."

Most people are a bit nervous when it comes to follow-up notes, so don't worry. Just keep it short, friendly, and use the above guidelines. It might not get you a job right away, but developing these connections over time will help you become very successful. Remember this: whether or not you get offered a job, you absolutely always want to keep the door open for future opportunities. That means showing interviewers you're prepared, being friendly and amiable during the interview, and sending nice follow-up notes to show your appreciation. It just may land you an incredible opportunity in the future.

That's about it for this section. We covered everything you need to know about the onsite interview, including how to prepare, how to knock it out of the park in the onsite itself, and how to set yourself up for success with thoughtful follow-ups. This section is meant to give you all the tools you need to be successful and get a great job offer, but keep in mind that there are a lot of variables outside of your control. You can't control who else is interviewing or how much experience they have. You can't change an interviewer's biases or preconceived notions about certain types of candidates. There are even some crazier things that affect your odds of success: what if the hiring manager had a tough conversation with their boss before the interview and is in an unforgiving mood? What if they had a bad lunch and are feeling ill?

You can't prevent these things or even wrap your head around all the potential factors affecting the outcome- all you can do is work hard to prepare and do your best during and after the interview. If you don't get the job, don't worry or take it personally- just do a postmortem and figure out how you'll get better, then move on. If you do get the role, congratulations! Clearly the hard work paid off.

Know this: you will succeed over time as long as you work hard to prepare, reflect on failures, improve, and be flexible in your approach. That's the only recipe for success that is reliable and works consistently. Focus on what you can control and improve every single day.

Week 8

As you can tell by now, it's not likely that your progress follows the exact timeline laid out in this guide. Some candidates find themselves doing onsite interviews in the first two weeks (as opposed to the 5th week), while some candidates take much longer to gain traction. Your mileage may vary, so don't be too worried if you're not where you want to be yet.

This section is about reflection. All too often we get lost in the maze of trying to find a new job, and we don't stop to think about our progress at a higher level. You must learn to analyze yourself and identify things that are holding you back. This is a crucial step in improving, potentially even more so than working hard. Some people work hard all the time, but don't bother to figure out how to get better, and they burn themselves out in the process. You need to "sharpen the saw". A guide can't tell you what you're doing wrong, but it can help you ask the right questions and figure out for yourself how you can get better and ultimately reach your goal.

Let's get started. The basic theme here is that you want to look at your progress from a higher perspective: if you were evaluating and coaching yourself, what would you say? How would you think about your performance? This is not meant to be a negative exercise, and some candidates are far too harsh with themselves. You want to think about the good things you've done, so you can keep doing those things, and also identify what areas of the job search need some work. Pro tip: do this in writing so it will become ingrained in your mind. Here are some questions to consider:

How do you feel about your performance overall? Regardless of whether or not you got a job offer, how was your effort? It's important to be honest with yourself when you're thinking about the effort you put in to your job search. Is this something you worked on every day, or at least most days? Or did you take two weeks off in the middle of the process? Think about what grade you'd give yourself, from F at the lowest to A+ at the highest. Remember, it's better to be honest and give yourself a B than it is to bend the truth and give yourself an A+.

Now that you have your grade, why did you earn that grade? If it's an A-, why is it an A-? Use bullet points here, and make sure your talk about the positives in addition to the negatives (if you didn't do anything at all, you'd give yourself an F, and you probably wouldn't have made it as far as this section anyway). The positives could read something like, "I made the list of jobs and worked my way from the least-desirable to the most-desirable. I also did outreach every day, and when I had an interview I practiced by writing the questions out and saying them out loud".

The "room for improvement section" might read something like, "I didn't keep up the outreach every week, and when I did outreach I only did online job applications. I only applied for jobs through connections once or twice, but I know I could have done more. Also, when I had my first data challenge, I kind of just jumped in on the first question and didn't read and understand the entire prompt".

It's important to think about what you could have done better, even if you got a job offer. Here's a secret to success: even the people who are the best in the world at what they do think about how they can get better. They're always improving, even when they win the championship or execute an amazing business deal. How do you think Amazon became such a massively successful company? Jeff Bezos didn't say, "Oh, looks like we're the best online bookstore in the world. I guess we did it- time to retire". He kept asking how the company could get better. He thought about what they could do to radically improve their results.

That's what you're doing right now. You're doing an analysis of your performance looking for ways to improve. If you spent two months trying to get a job in data, but didn't get one- don't worry- you're not alone. Plenty of candidates take even longer than that. The fact that you tried to get a job but didn't get quite there should be totally motivating for you and you should be excited to learn and improve. Life is about growth. Finding a job is about learning (through resources like this chapter), making attempts, and learning from those attempts. As long as you're putting forth a good effort and learning from your results, you're succeeding.

Here are some more questions to ask yourself:

- Did I follow the instructions in the guide? Why or why not? In what ways could I have done better following the strategy?

- How was your level of outreach? Did you truly stretch yourself and reach out to connections, and connections of connections? Or did you say, "Oh, I shouldn't bother that person. We only worked together for a year and we're not exactly close friends". Think about how you could have created more opportunities for yourself, again, even if you ultimately received a job offer.

- What grade would you give yourself for interview preparation? Did you do your research? What about writing your answers down and practicing out loud? If you didn't, I can bet you didn't end up with the ideal outcome. What would you do differently next time?

- Was there anything in this strategy guide that proved to be incorrect? This is important. This is a fantastic section and a lot of hard work went into making it the best possible strategy for getting a job in data, but we can't pretend it's the gospel. Some parts may not work for everyone, and that's OK. Did you notice anything, and if so how would you change or modify your approach?

Make sure to write down the answers to these questions so they become ingrained in your mind. You want to really learn this stuff and improve next time- it's better to get a D- and learn from it than it is to get a B and not learn it (and most of the time a B isn't enough to get you your dream job).

Conclusion

Did you find this section useful? Did you follow the process outlined? If you did, you've either got a great job in data or are on your way to getting one. This has been a comprehensive look at what it takes to get your career started in this field, and hopefully it has been useful to you. Remember that this is not going to be your last job search, so let's review a few things:

First, a big part of the process is having the right plan in place. This chapter is your plan, and you can supplement it in any way you think would be helpful. Maybe you'd like to incorporate weekly coffee meetings with someone already in the world of data to get their feedback, or maybe you'd just like to take things a step further and have a friend "mock interview" you when you've got something lined up. Whether you do those things or just stick with the plan laid out in this chapter, the right strategy is going to help you find your way to success.

As we've mentioned before, there are a lot of uncontrollables when it comes to getting a job, particularly when it's a new field for you. Reflecting on your outcomes, learning, and coming up with a plan for implementation is absolutely within your control, and that's the secret of people who really succeed. You've got the plan. You're going to implement it. And, you're probably going to skin your knee here and there- you're going to mess up an interview, fail a data challenge, and probably not get the offer after an onsite. It's OK! Let this be your mantra: persevere intelligently. Don't just keep trying the same stuff over and over again. Reflect on your process as what you could have done better. See yourself from the third person, as if you were a totally different person analyzing your actions. What holes do you see? What could be done better? Don't forget to ask yourself positive questions too: what did you do right? What should you keep doing in the future? What were the success you did have, and what actions led you to those successes?

Asking yourself these questions and answering them is how you'll win over time, regardless of whether or not you're lucky, have the right degree, have the right background, or anything else. Constant improvement is how you win, and it's within your control. Persist and be positive. Persevere intelligently. Try, learn, improve, and try again. You can do it.

Top Questions from Real Interviews

In this section we're going to go into full detail about the thing that is on every job candidate's mind: what questions will I be asked, and how do I answer them? Not only will we tell you the answers to these questions, but we'll also go deep and get into what the interviewer is really asking and what they want to know.

The knowledge in this section comes from incredible experience- many years and hundreds of interviews from both sides of the interview table, so you'll get a complete perspective of each question. If you pay attention and absorb the concepts in this section, you'll undoubtedly do well in the most critical part of finding a new job and land a role you'll really love. Let's get down to business.

This section is organized very simply. We have a section for each question, and in each section we'll break down the most important information you need to understand: who will ask the question, what they're really asking, and what they really want to know. Remember that interview questions are almost always a little more than what's on the surface.

For example, do you think that when a hiring manager asks, "Tell me about yourself", that they want to know that you like to work out several days a week and occasionally watch HBO? Definitely not. There's more than meets the eye in that question, and others. Let the information in this section be the secret key that unlocks a true understanding of what interviewers want to know, and how you can actually connect with them and show you're a good fit.

What you need to do is read this chapter carefully and take notes. If anything is surprising or counterintuitive, make a note of it. Also, don't forget to read the last section, where we'll get into how you prepare and really maximize your effectiveness- because it's really not enough to just know what questions are going to be asked. Let's dive in.

Tell me about yourself

This question will likely come from a hiring manager, but can also be asked by a recruiter. You'll get asked this earlier in the interview process (typically during phone interviews).

What they're really asking

This question is definitely asking about your work, but more about how you got to where you are, rather than details about your current role. They're asking you to give a miniature version of your life story, but focused more on your work and career. If you're interviewing for your first role out of college, it should still be focused on what you've done to get yourself ready for a great career.

Note that they're not asking you to talk about your hobbies, what you do on weekends, your family, or your pet snake. Sometimes interviewers do want to get to know you a little bit in that way, but if they do they'll ask a question like, "What do you do outside of work". This question is about your work and career.

What they really want to know

This is one of the first questions asked, so at this point recruiters or hiring managers are just interested in knowing a few things. First, they want to get a feel for your ability to have a conversation, ie. can you give a clear, sensical answer and not drone on and on or say something strange. Don't worry about this- giving clear answers is easy and we'll show you how.

They also want to know that you've grown and progressed in your work life. Where have you shown initiative? How have you challenged yourself?

Recruiters and hiring managers want to know that you can learn and make progress, which is something everyone has to do when they start a new role (particularly if they're breaking into the field of data).

How to answer

If this question seems daunting, don't worry- this is actually one of the easier questions to answer. Before we jump in, based on what you've read above, how would you answer this? Go ahead and take a minute and give your full response, out loud if you can.

Now let's go through some recommendations and start to formulate the perfect answer. Remember that, like everything else in this strategy guide, this information is based on our experience as both candidates and hiring managers, as well as information we've gathered by talking with candidates, hiring managers, and recruiters. We've had a lot of failures and a lot of success answering all of these questions, so rest assured that you're getting the full benefit of what we know.

First, before brainstorming how you want to answer a question, make a list of what you want to communicate. This is an incredibly helpful step that will help you create great responses and put you ahead of the pack. Here is an example from one candidate, interviewing from a Data Scientist role:

- I have done challenging and important work

- I have sought creative ways to solve problems

- I have challenged myself to build skills to solve those problems

If you were a hiring manager, how would you feel about hiring someone with these traits? Probably pretty great- these are great attributes for anyone in any role to possess. Think about what you want to communicate, but make it a relatively short list (3 items is usually enough).

Now, let's think about our response in light of the things we'd like to communicate, continuing to use the above as an example. For each item, write a sentence from your work or college history that applies. It can be specific, because you're going to be asked about projects and other details later.

- I have done challenging and important work

Example: I started at {Company} in a marketing role, first working on email campaigns and then gradually working on bigger and bigger projects.

- I have sought creative ways to solve problems

While in that role, I noticed that our work would get delayed if an analyst was out sick or if there was turnover, because we needed lots of data for marketing. I decided to take it upon myself to learn how to get that data.

- I have challenged myself to build skills to solve those problems

I taught myself SQL by taking online courses, reading books, and working with other analysts in the company. After getting comfortable there, I expanded into Python and started automating our workflows, which is saving us a lot of time.

Does that make sense? When you answer open-ended questions (any of them), you want to make no more than 2-3 clear, concise points, illustrated with examples. Now, let's string these together to form a complete answer:

Interviewer: "Why don't we start with you telling me a little bit about yourself?"

You: "Sure, no problem. I started at {Company} in a marketing role. It's been a great experience because I started with basic email campaigns, and gradually worked on bigger and bigger projects, even leading some of them. While in the role I noticed that our work would get delayed if an analyst was out sick or if there was turnover, because we needed lots of data for marketing. I decided to learn how to get the data myself by teaching myself SQL. I took online courses, read books, and collaborated with other analysts in the company. After getting comfortable with SQL, I expanded Python and am excited to say we're now automating many of our workflows, which is a huge time-saver."

Notice that the wording is a bit different than the individual points above- this is intentional. It is very important that you start with the points you want to communicate and really know those well, then practice giving complete answers. For this question and others, always start with what you want to communicate- start at a high level and fill in the details.

Where a lot of candidates mess up is when they'll do some research online for interview questions, write out their answers, and practice the answers verbatim- but they don't think about the points they're trying to communicate. When it comes time to actually be in an interview and answer the questions, their mind goes blank and they say maybe half their answer (and it's not very good). Has this ever happened to you? Thankfully you have this approach now and know what you need to do to be successful.

Tell me about your current role

You'll probably get asked this a few times- usually first by the recruiter in the initial phone screen. Be prepared to answer this question for any hiring manager interview, as well as any non-technical interviews you have with the company.

What they're really asking

"Tell me about your role" is one of the more transparent questions we'll cover in this chapter. Here, the hiring manager or recruiter does truly want to know about your current role, but there's one question you should ask yourself: if the recruiter or hiring manager has your resume, which has your current role and some bullet points you've included, so why would they ask you this?

Simple answer- they want more context. They want to hear how you think about and explain your job. Most candidates fluff up their resumes and descriptions, so the hiring team wants to hear about your work in your own words.

What they really want to know

First, they want to know that you can speak to your current role clearly. You need to be able to explain what you do in clear, precise language. This is a challenge for some people, especially those who wear many hats at work. They're often tempted to say something like, "Oh, I do a little bit of everything..." and then gloss over some of the basics of their work. Unfortunately, this is a poor strategy- it may seem counterintuitive but nobody wants to hire someone who, "does a little bit of everything". It's OK if you have a lot of responsibilities, but you want to be clear and emphasize the major parts of your role and the parts that apply to the role you're interviewing for.

They also want to know that you've done work that's important to your current company. Most questions are about the recruiter or hiring manager trying to understand your value, and one of the best proxies for how valuable you'll be to their company is how valuable you are to your current company. Do you manage people or lead important projects? Are you the go-to person in a certain area of expertise? These are all things that demonstrate high value, but even if you're not "the best" at anything in particular, you're still valuable. How do we know you're valuable? Because your company pays you to be there. It doesn't matter if you're making cold calls or running a division or sweeping the floor- remember that you do have value and show the hiring team.

How to answer

The two main things you want to emphasize when answering this question are that you do valuable work at your current company, and the work you do is relevant to the role you're applying for. For most people the latter is tricky if they're trying to break into the field of data, but if understand what the new role is looking for and think about all the different parts of your current job, you should be able to find some similarities. Let's separate out our points and add some hypothetical context. For illustration we'll assume this is for a Data Scientist role, and the job description mentions user conversion analysis.

The work I do is valuable to my current company.

I lead many of our marketing initiatives which are the primary way we acquire new customers. I focus on figuring out which programs are most effective and with this data I recommend strategies based on where I think our money is best spent.

The work I do is relevant to the role I'm applying for.

In order to determine the most effective marketing efforts, I spend time analyzing and thinking about the conversion channel, particularly for email marketing. This involves looking at the number of emails we sent (minus the bounce rate), our open rate, our click through rate, and ultimately our conversion to a customer. This allows us to optimize each step of the funnel and produce really effective marketing campaigns.

This is all it really takes. The last section in this chapter will go over high-level tips, but by now you're getting the hang of it: figure out the 2-3 things you'd like to communicate, and do so with clear, concise statements that get to the point quickly. Don't overthink it. You don't have to explain everything in one go because you'll probably be asked follow-up questions.

What are you looking for in your next role?

This is another question you're likely to hear a few times, most likely by both the recruiter and hiring manager. The good news is that you can have pretty much the same response for both interviewers, since they're looking for the same things.

What they're really asking

They're really asking- does this person actually want to work in this role and at this company, and is it for good reasons? Good reasons are that you're looking for more challenge and growth, you're looking to work with best-in-class data teams, and/or that you love the company/product and are interested in tackling tricky problems. Bad reasons are that you're looking for better pay (yes, candidates say this) or something generic like "I'm looking to do more analytical work" (duh).

What they really want to know

The main thing the hiring team wants to know with this question is that you actually want to do the role you're applying for. It may sound crazy, but there are a lot of candidates who will apply to and interview for a role that has nothing to do with their aspirations or even work they're interested in.

For example, we've seen candidates apply for Business Analyst roles that are very straightforward analytics roles involving lots of SQL, Python, business strategy, dashboarding, etc. While these are great roles, sometimes when we ask candidates what they're looking for in their next role they respond with things like, "I'd love to work on Machine Learning problems, and I've been working on Neural Nets in my spare time so I'd love to tackle those sorts of projects." At that point we know it's pretty much a non-starter.

Thoughts from a Hiring Manager

"The last thing I want is to hire someone for a role they don't want because that is a recipe for dissatisfaction on both sides. Even if my team is really under the gun and we need someone ASAP, I just can't bring myself to hire someone as a Data Analyst if they really want to be an ML Engineer, or anything else that is a mismatch. I know that even if they say they want to do the role and have all the ability in the world, I know they won't be happy long-term if they're looking for a completely different role"

Let's be clear- it's OK to aspire to different and more challenging work. After all, most people need a few foundational roles (such as Data Analyst) if they want to eventually work up to harder technical problems or management. The question is asking what you're looking for in your next role, so articulate that clearly. State your 2-3 main points, and if you'd like it's OK to add something like, "Long-term I think I'd look to work into Machine Learning problems, and potentially Neural Nets". This, combined with your other answers, shows that you're looking to grow and contribute more to the next company you join.

How to answer

What are the main points we want to articulate? Your exact answers may vary, but let's dive right in using a Product Analyst role at Uber as an example.

I'm excited about this role, specifically

I'm excited about the Product Analyst role because I've always enjoyed working with Product- both digging into current products and using data to think about the strategic direction of how we interact with consumers.

I'm excited about this company, specifically

I'm interested in this opportunity specifically because I'm an avid Uber user, and I've always been interested in the different types of problems to solve. From things like Rider Wait Time to New Driver Acquisition, I feel like this is a role and company where I could both learn a lot and contribute the knowledge I've gained in my current role to help drive the product forward.

What do we notice? The answer is specific to both the company and the role, and demonstrates general enthusiasm for the work. We know that this person is truly interested in this opportunity and likely won't be looking to jump to a different job soon after they're hired. This answer is short and sweet, but still articulates enough information for the recruiter or hiring manager to feel good about their candidacy.

Tell me about one of your projects

This question is definitely more common in hiring manager interviews, but also pops up in recruiter interviews occasionally. Hiring managers like to ask follow-up questions for this one, so be prepared to speak to details about your work.

What they're really asking

Here the recruiter or hiring manager is really asking, "Tell me about one of your important projects that made a real contribution to the company." Again, they're asking about the relevance of your current work and the value you bring to the table. They're asking themselves, "Can this candidate do the work of the role I'm hiring for? Can they make meaningful contributions to this company without too much training and ramp-up?"

What they really want to know

The hiring team wants to know a few things. Number one, that you've worked on significant value-generating projects in your current role. They want to know that you're trusted with important work and can execute when it's time to produce results.

They also want to know that you can overcome challenges and barriers. Almost all projects have roadblocks, so don't hesitate to call those out and talk about how you navigated to a great outcome. This is your time to show that you will be effective with whatever they task you with. Bonus points if you illustrate how you collaborated with others and used your soft skills to help get things done- "I stayed up all night working on XYZ" is OK at best (but is probably detrimental)- show that you were able to work collaboratively with others to get the job done and they'll be impressed.

How to answer

Yet again, think about what you want to communicate that will generally align with what the recruiter or hiring manager wants to know about you when they ask this question. Put simply, you want to illustrate that you work on important value-adding projects to the company, and you also understand how to work through problems to achieve a positive outcome.

Additionally, since we're talking about a project, let's try incorporating something new. it's called the SCORE framework, and was originally introduced by McKinsey & Company, one of the top consulting firms in the world. SCORE stands for Situation, Conflict, Resolution (don't ask why they had to add the additional letters). Let's try an example:

Situation: Our email marketing campaigns are one of the top channels for for new customer acquisition, and last quarter we were getting ready for our biggest email push of the year.

Conflict: One of our major blockers for marketing campaigns would be when our marketing analyst was out sick, too busy, or otherwise couldn't help with list pulls or analyses.

Resolution: I anticipated that the analyst not being available to help and decided to take it into my own hands. Because I had a few months until the big email push, I started teaching myself SQL and really getting immersed in how we pull and analyze data by collaborating with other analysts. When it came time to launch the campaign, and later analyze it, I was actually able to handle all of the data needs myself and ensure that we could execute the launch without any delays. It ended up being our most successful marketing campaign in several years, and now we're set up to be a self-sufficient marketing team while still having other analytical resources when we need them.

This isn't the only way to answer the question, but we're bringing up the SCORE framework because most candidates struggle not because they haven't done relevant or important projects, but because they don't understand how to articulate the details of a project clearly. Many candidates either don't give enough information or get into the weeds and tell a long, winding story without much of a point. Clear, concise communication wins the day.

Why ___ company?

You could hear this question from anyone you interview with, and it's very prevalent in recruiter phone screens as well as cross-functional or fit/culture interviews. This should be one of the easier questions to answer, since you're at least somewhat interested in the company if you're interviewing.

What they're really asking

They're really asking, "Does this person actually want to work here, or do they just want a job? Do they even know what we do and/or are they a user of our product?". They're trying to get a sense of how you feel about the company, and how much you know about what they do.

What they want to know

It's important that recruiters and hiring managers know you're interested in the company itself, because they're going to spend a lot of time and money to train and ramp up whomever they hire, and they want to make sure that person is going to stick around. They don't want to hire someone who is looking for a stepping-stone job or someone who is going to get bored and leave in a year. They want someone who's in it for the long term, and part of that is a solid interest in the company.

They also want to know that you'll be happy if you get the job, and part of that is how much you like the company. If you feel that you work at a company with an amazing product and team, then it's a lot more likely that you'll be happy and stay happy. It's difficult to work with people who have no interest in the company because although many times they're competent and a good performer, they don't have much "juice" or energy to do really outstanding work. Just about every hiring manager would rather that a great data professional leave the company and go do something they really enjoy than have them stick around and be dissatisfied.

How to answer

This should be pretty simple, but maybe a different phrasing would be helpful. If you think about why you want to work at XYZ company, you initial thoughts may be that it's a great brand, or the role is a big step up, or even that you think the perks would be awesome. Those are absolutely OK to think, but they probably won't help you answer this question effectively.

Try answering this question instead: what do you respect about XYZ company? If interviewing for a Data Scientist role within Google Maps, you might say, "Well I think it's a fantastic product, and it's my understanding that Google has the best data scientists in the world. I use Google Maps for everything from biking directions to restaurant recommendations, so I'd love to work on this product and tackle interesting problems. I'm interested in Google because it would be a great opportunity for me to both learn from some of the best minds in data and also contribute my talent to help the product grow."

It's a good exercise to think about how typical interview questions might be rephrased. There can be a lot of "whys" to why you want to work at a company, and there's nothing wrong with pay and perks playing a part.

But when you think about what you genuinely respect about a company and can articulate that, it gets hiring teams excited to bring you on.

How to Implement the Master Plan

Now that we're done going through the top five questions, let's take a step back and think about how you should approach answering these and any other questions that come up. The candidates who do the best and ultimately get the best job offers almost always have a structured approach to answering interview questions.

Before you even start to answer a question, ask yourself those two questions: what are they really asking, and what do they want to know? While it's true you won't know exactly what is on someone's mind, try to think generally. They want someone who adds value, will be good at the job, is interested in the role specifically, wants to work at the company specifically, etc. As you're using this chapter and researching more interview questions, think about these two questions first.

Two things you need to keep in mind (write them down right now): Clear and Concise. You should strive to have everything you say or write to be clear and concise. Clear: is what I'm saying easy to understand? Am I getting my point across? Is it easy to figure out exactly what my point is? Concise: am I getting to the point quickly? Am I answering without a long-winded story? Am I using no more than 2-3 clear points? Most candidates focus only on what they're going to say, rather than how they're going to say it- clear and concise is a major tip that will put you far ahead of the pack.

On that note, part of your approach for brainstorming answers to interview questions should be to write out the 2-3 things you'd like to communicate. Never start by writing or typing a full-paragraph answer to the question. Ask yourself, "What do I want to say? What do I want to communicate?" Once you have your 2-3 points, add context relevant to the question (eg. about a project you've worked on). Then, string it all together to make a clear and concise answer. Don't go on forever, but you don't have to be super brief- say what you need to say.

Some final tips: smile during interviews, even if you're on the phone. People like to be around people who are happy and engaged, and it energizes them. Show that you're enthusiastic about the role and company. If you can't get excited in the interview stage, how will you feel when you're actually in the role? Don't go crazy, but don't be afraid to show that you're excited.

That's it for this chapter. We recommend reading through it once first, then giving it another detailed read when you're preparing for your interviews. The great part about the content we've given you is that the ideas and approach will easily transfer to other interview questions. Read this chapter, know what you want to communicate, and practice, and you'll be in great shape.

Expanded Questions

Alright, now it's your turn to go through the process. We've combed through our own data and research and are providing another 15 questions from real interviews- make sure these are in your repertoire.

Remember that there are three questions you need to ask yourself when preparing for a particular interview question: What are they really asking? What do they really want to know? How should I answer? In answering the last question, you'll also want to write down what you want to communicate, which should align with what they really want to know.

This approach is crucial for getting into the rhythm of answering interview questions because you're not going to be able to memorize all possible answers, and even if you could it wouldn't be a good idea. Let's get started.

What's important to you when you're looking at companies?

Do you understand how our business works?

How will this role take you to your goals?

Tell me about a time when you had to make a decision without all of the information

How do you deal with data skepticism from non-technical people?

How do you communicate with up-level stakeholders?

Why are you leaving your current company?

What is some feedback you've received, both positive and constructive?

Tell me about a time you failed

Tell me about a time you had to approach something in a structured way

Tell me about a time you weren't able to collaborate effectively with a cross-functional partner

What's your process for getting information out of a cross-functional partner?

What does your team do?

Explain a technical concept related to [role you're applying for]

How would you explain [XYZ concept] to a Product Manager without a technical background?

Scraps to SQL

A major inspiration for creating the Learn Data strategy guides has been all of the incredible success stories we've heard from people who were able to break into the field of data and get their dream job. The entire process can sometimes feel like an impossible mountain to climb, but once you reach your goals it feels amazing. We wanted to make sure we did not leave out examples of success, so we're giving you a transcript of an interview with someone who was probably like you, and ultimately became very successful in this industry.

When conducting these interviews we wanted to make sure to get you as much information as possible, especially around compensation, and thankfully this data pro was willing to tell us. Since we discussed sensitive matters, his only request was that we keep him anonymous.

Interview transcription

Tell us about your current role

Right now I'm a Data Scientist at a mid-sized tech company in the Bay Area that recently IPO'd. I got in a little before the IPO but not very early. I love my job- it involves a lot of analytics and I get to collaborate with Product Managers and other Data Scientists on a regular basis. The day-to-day involves a lot of SQL querying and a good amount of Python to dig into how our key product is performing in terms of general KPIs as well as the underlying health of the product (eg., looking at outages). It's a fun job. I'm on a team with really smart Data Scientists and I enjoy working for my boss.

How did your career start? What did you study in college?

It wasn't that glamorous at the beginning. I started as a Sales Development Representative at a tech company here in SF. I feel like I got lucky because I applied to a ton of different companies after I finished college and barely even got interviews, let alone job offers. To this day I'm really surprised they hired me, but I'm grateful too.

The job was OK, but not exactly the type of work that gets you out of bed in the morning. A sales development representative is basically a person who cold calls potential clients, explains the product, and tries to set a meeting. When you do set a meeting, you hand the info over to the account executive who then tries to close the deal. Overall the job was a bit of a grind, but there were some good people there and it was not a bad gig.

My Bachelor's degree is just in Management- pretty generic. I had lots of different types of classes in college and consider myself pretty eclectic. Like most people I had no idea what I wanted to do while I was in college, so I just signed up for a major and read books on the side to feed my interest. I think ultimately I wanted to start my own business.

How did you feel about the sales role? Did you enjoy it?

I would say yes and no. There were definitely times when I really enjoyed it, especially if I was having lots of success. As I mentioned before, the people were great to work with and I made some good friends. The company itself was cool and we had some decent perks.

There were some downsides though. It was a lot of hours and hard work, which I don't mind, but I often questioned what all the work was ultimately leading to. Was I going to stay in sales forever? Did I even want to? So there were the more long-term questions like that and the fact that I didn't really enjoy the work itself. Making phone calls all day, trying to convince people to set up a meeting, getting rejected, all of that. For some people it's fine but I just didn't like it.

The pay was OK. When I first started I was making barely enough to get by in the Bay Area, but after I started earning commission there was a little more wiggle room. Either way it definitely wasn't helping me move towards my financial goals and I didn't see a path to earn enough for the things I wanted like to own my own home.

If you don't mind answering, how much money were you making in that role?

My starting base salary was $40,000 a year. At my best I think I earned $50,000 after commission. That is a great salary in a lot of places but the cost of living is very high in the Bay Area. I would definitely say that part of the reason I got into to data was my motivation to earn more money, among other things).

What happened after that role? Did you go straight into the Data Scientist role?

Not quite. After a while I was considering quitting, but then I saw a Marketing Coordinator position open up. I wasn't crazy about marketing or anything, but it sounded like a better option than getting another sales role at another company. I talked to my boss and she supported me wanting to pursue that role (it's always better to move someone within a company than let them quit) and put in a good word for me.

The interview process was tough and I had to put in a lot of extra hours, but ultimately I got the job. I was excited- I hadn't been enjoying my work in sales and I was excited to move on to something new.

What was that role that like? Did you work with data?

Well, it was pretty basic. I was in charge of our email and direct mail marketing (direct mail is just physical mail). My main tasks were to figure which potential customers we were going to target, get the email list from our analyst, write the marketing copy, set up the email campaign in our marketing software, and review the results with my boss after the campaign had time to run and our analyst analyzed the performance. From there we would determine whether or not it worked and decide on the next best course of action.

Initially I would say I was "around" data more than I actually worked with it. I would ask the analyst for data, take the spreadsheet, and then put it in marketing software. That was basically it. Originally I didn't do any sort of real processing or analysis on the data.

How did you learn to automate your work?

Well, I didn't actually get my start automating- that came a little later. I got into the world of data sort of accidentally- there was a situation where we were on a tight deadline and needed the email lists so we could send out a campaign right away. Unfortunately our analyst was on vacation, and the person who usually covers for him was also on vacation.

This was not good. We had to basically run around asking other analysts if they could help pull this list- and most of them were either too busy or not familiar enough with marketing data sources to help. Eventually we got someone to pull the list, but it was super stressful and we had to call in a lot of favors.

I'll never forget when I got the Excel doc from the analyst who ended up helping us- it was just a list of emails. It always looked like that, but this time was different. I looked at it and thought, "Why can't I just do this?"

What happened after that?

I didn't know much about how it all worked, but I did know that the analyst mainly used SQL to pull the data. I decided to learn the basics before jumping into anything at work, so I spent a weekend watching videos and reading up on the topic. I think I may have used Coursera at some point in the very beginning, but I'm not sure- thankfully SQL is applied in pretty much the same way for most data needs, so the stuff I was reading applied everywhere.

My goal at the very beginning was just to be able to "speak the language", meaning I just wanted to be able to understand what the analyst was doing when he showed me. I knew that I wasn't going to turn into an expert overnight. After a weekend of studying and research I felt comfortable and asked our analyst to show me how he got the data. He was really nice and happy to take some time to show me everything and answer my questions.

Eventually I got set up with access to the databases and basically just started writing SQL code. For me it really helps to "learn by doing", and this was especially the case with SQL. I picked up a reference book so I could look up concepts such as conditional querying, but beyond that I just worked through our actual data.

Long story short, before long I was able to write pretty good SQL and get our email list data without having to go through our analyst. My boss was impressed and asked if there were any other analytical task I could take on, so I told him what I thought I could handle and gradually built up the number of SQL tasks I was doing.

Additionally there were some analyses in Excel that I thought would be good to get familiar with. It was basic stuff to analyze the performance of our marketing campaigns, but it involved a lot of manual work. The analyst taught me how to do everything and at a certain point it was transitioned over to me completely. After a while of going through the manual process of analyzing this data I had that classic thought- "There must be a better way". I discovered that Python is great for automating tasks, and the rest is history.

How did you build skills from there?

I initially learned Python by reading, "Automate the Boring Stuff". That was a great way to pick up the language and immediately go into automating the marketing analysis. Once I did that, I wanted to learn more, so I took a Data Science program on Coursera. It took me a few months, and I think I paid around $50 per month. I didn't really plan my educational path all that well but I got lucky with Coursera. If I could go back, I definitely would have planned it out a bit more thoughtfully- I didn't really know which direction I wanted to go in in terms of my career.

Why did you choose an online learning platform instead of teaching yourself again?

I thought about teaching myself again and even bought a book or two, but the reality was that didn't know what I didn't know. I knew that I wanted to go deeper in the data world, but it was difficult to determine which concepts I needed to learn without having a small, solvable problem. It was much simpler with the marketing analysis automation, for example- I knew what I wanted to do and already had a way to do the task without Python, so it was much easier to translate that into Google searches and things to look up in a book. An example would be, "How do you sum rows in Python?". From there you're just learning syntax and concepts that apply to your problem.

When I wanted to branch out, however, it was different. I didn't know what I didn't know. Part of my motivation was that I wanted to do more technical work and grow my skills more. I got lucky and got to work with some of the Product Managers at my company, and I was always interested in product. I learned that product Data Scientist roles existed and started doing my research- from there I knew that's what I wanted to pursue.

What was the job search like?

I tried applying to some roles and basically got nowhere. I felt like I was being reasonable and applying to things within reach, but I wasn't even getting recruiter calls. I asked an older friend of mine to look at my resume and talked about the challenges I was facing. He said that I wasn't likely to get any call backs because my role title was "Marketing Coordinator" and I didn't have anything on my resume showing that I did data analysis. He recommended that since I was learning new material anyway I should try to get some kind of credential, even if it was just an online program.

I browsed around Coursera and found a program that looked like would be good. I wasn't quite sure what I needed exactly, so I took a Data Science course that used Python. It was pretty challenging but I pushed through it and learned a lot.

It took me a few months to complete that. Once I felt comfortable with my knowledge, I put the program on my resume and started applying. It was pretty scattered, but I did have a list of companies I wanted to work at. Even with the credential and a polished resume, I still struggled to get interviews.

Is there anything you would do differently next time you look for a job?

For sure. Looking back, I was really disorganized. I had a spreadsheet of jobs and whatnot but I didn't really have much of a plan. I just knew I wanted to get a job in data and started applying. I liked the material in the Get Hired in 8 Weeks section- it is definitely something I wish I had, or I wish I at least had some kind of plan or insider info on how it all works.

How many offers did you get? Were you able to negotiate the the pay?

I have a great job and I'm thankful for it, but if I planned it better I think I would have had more options to choose from. When I was offered the Data Scientist role it was the only role I was offered, but I think it would have been good to have multiple offers.

I didn't have a ton of leverage, but I negotiated the pay anyway. I learned something important- even though I didn't have a bunch of competing offers, I still had a job- so that was leverage. I always had the alternative to stay at a job I liked and continue working on my skills.

What made you finally decide to accept the offer from the company you went with?

Well, at first I over thought it. I thought about all the reasons why it was good and why it wasn't good, and I spent time thinking about what else might be out there. In the end, it was a role in data as a Data Scientist that I was very excited about, it was a step up in pay, and I felt confident about the company itself. Ultimately I just went for it and now I feel great about my decision.

How what is the pay difference between the two roles? Can you give us details?

It's significant. Of course both jobs had good benefits that roughly equalled out, and for my new company the commute is actually a bit shorter, which is a huge plus. As a Marketing Coordinator I made roughly $60k/yr, and then maybe another $10k in stock grants if it was a good year. The Data Scientist role I accepted was about $150k/yr all-in. Huge difference. Obviously there's more to it than money but being able to take my income to the next level is something I'm really proud of and it's going to help me take care of my family as well as allow me to do the things I want to do.

What's next for you?

I'm not sure yet. I've been in my role for a while, but I still feel like I have a lot to learn. I'm just kind of staying in the moment. I find that whenever I focus too much on the future and "what's next", I lose sight of why I wanted to do this kind of work in the first place. I think I'll have a lot of options, and for now I'm happy doing the work, getting paid, and learning a lot.

We have a large audience of people aspiring to be data professionals and make their way in this world- any advice for them?

I've read through the stuff in these guides and it seems great- I'd say go ahead and stick with this material since you've got it. Other than that I would say that the job hunt is difficult and you just need to keep trying. Keep learning, keep going for jobs, and repeat the cycle. I have a lot of friends that work in data and tech and I've never heard anyone say that finding a job was easy, so don't worry if it seems hard for you. It's tough for everyone, but the results are worth it.

Essential Data Reading List

In our research and interviews with data professionals, both in the field and aspiring, one common thread we came across is that they're all consistently learning. Data Science as a profession is very broad, and there are always avenues to explore if you're looking to up your skills. One simple way to do that is through picking up a book on a technical topic and getting into the details. There are other ways too, such as taking additional online courses, but one of the key advantages of a book is that it's on your shelf and can serve as a reference literally any time you need it. With online courses, you'll probably have to dig through your notes and re-watch videos to find a specific topic, while a book will have an index that you can use to find things quickly. Whether you're just starting out or further along in your career, this is incredibly valuable.

Below we've assembled five books that are highly recommended by data pros, and are mostly aimed at those who are earlier in their career. Unless you're a complete expert in SQL, Python, and Machine Learning, the below books will serve as an incredible resource for years to come.

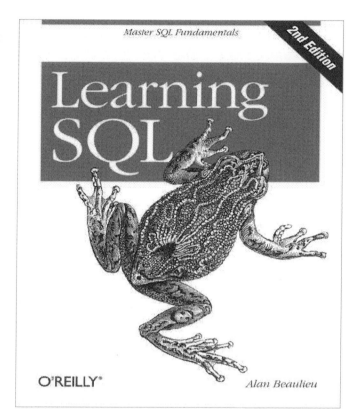

Learning SQL

Amazon Link

Level: Beginner

For all the talk about Machine Learning and AI, one of
the most overlooked skills in any data professional's
toolkit is SQL. For those unfamiliar, SQL is a language
that allows you to retrieve data from the company's data
stores using commands such as SELECT, FROM, and
WHERE. With some skill in SQL, you're able to get the
data you need quickly, and leave out everything you don't
need using filters.

We won't get into depth about SQL here, but know that this is an extremely important skill. We haven't heard of any role in data that doesn't involve SQL on some level, and most companies test for it in the interview. The good news is that it's pretty easy to learn. "Learning SQL" is a great intro to the language, but will also serve as a reference guide for more advanced topics as you move through your career. It is highly recommended to keep at least one SQL book on the shelf, and "Learning SQL" is the perfect place to start.

Automate the Boring Stuff with Python

Amazon Link

Book Website

Level: Beginner

Now we're moving on to Python, and "Automate the Boring Stuff" is a classic text and an example that looks can be deceiving. Depending on who you are, automating pieces of your work may or may not be interesting, and may or may not even apply to your job, but this is worth picking up and reading nonetheless.

"Automate the Boring Stuff" provides a fantastic intro to the Python language. The first few chapters are devoted to the basics of Python: data structures, syntax, functions, etc., which will be the foundation of your programming knowledge. Additionally, it's important to know that Python is the top language for data analytics and data science, so at some point you'll want to become fluent.

The book covers not only the basics of Python, but also digs into how you can use it to automate routine tasks such as filling out forms, reading spreadsheets, and sending emails. For many students this is their first big, "A ha!" moment- when they realize just how powerful and seemingly magical the language can be.

Python Crash Course

Amazon Link

Level: Beginner

"Python Crash Course" is another classic introductory Python book. This is different from "Automate the Boring Stuff" in that it doesn't approach the language from the lens of automation, but rather focuses on giving you a taste of several potential applications of Python, including data visualization, creating games, and even building web applications.

Naturally, there are several sections covering the basics of Python, so this book will work well if you're looking for a solid introduction to Python. The real strength, however, is that the bulk of the text is focused on walking you through small, self-contained projects that help you build competency and confidence in your ability to code Python. Projects are a must and one of the best ways to learn a coding language because you have a concrete, achievable end vision you're working towards. This will motivate you to work through problems and find solutions, which will help grow your overall skill set.

Python for Data Analysis

Amazon Link

Level: Intermediate

Once you're comfortable with the basics of Python, you'll want to move on to more meaty topics. "Python for Data Analysis" is a favorite among many in Data Analyst, Data Science, and even Data Engineering career paths because it is a comprehensive guide to processing and analyzing data in Python. What most people find out when they're entering the world of data is that a lot of the work is pulling and cleaning data- this book will give you the skills to excel in this part of the job and will serve as a reference for the rest of your career.

The bulk of this book is focused on Pandas, one of the most popular Python libraries. Pandas allows you to quickly and efficiently process large datasets using the "DataFrame" data structure- this is a core piece of the data professional's toolkit.

In case you need another reason to pick this one up, here's one: the author of the book, Wes McKinney, is also the original author of Pandas itself. What better expert is there?

Data Science from Scratch

Amazon Link

Level: Intermediate

Naturally this book is a great starting place for the aspiring Data Scientists, but Engineers, Analysts, and anyone else who will potentially collaborate with Data Scientists should consider picking it up. The author, Joel Grus, has a career path that many seek to emulate- first starting as an Analyst at several companies, and eventually working on advanced Machine Learning and Software Engineering at Google.

Beyond the resume, he really knows Data Science and articulates it well. This book contains all the basics you need to get started in Data Science- beginning with the basics of visualizing data and linear algebra, working up to statistical concepts and hypothesis testing, and eventually even digging into Machine Learning and concepts such as Neural Networks. With this breadth of material you won't go very deep into any one topic, but it's a great introduction and will help you build foundational knowledge in Data Science.

One of the reasons we avoided hesitated to recommend this book historically was that the first edition was in Python 2, and the author went out of his way to say something like, "the Data Science community is firmly rooted in Python 2, so you should be too...." We disagreed. Thankfully, a new edition of "Data Science from Scratch" has been released, and it's all written in Python 3- definitely make sure you're getting the 2nd edition when you get this book.

The Hundred-Page Machine Learning Book

Amazon Link

Level: Intermediate/Advanced

This is the most recently-written entrant on this list, but also one of the most respected. A quick glance at the Amazon reviews shows that the response from the data community has been glowing, and this is destined to go down as a classic text for anyone looking to enter the world of Data Science and Machine Learning.

"The Hundred-Page Machine Learning Book" is different than other materials you're likely considering or have already consumed. Rather than a tutorial with lots of hands-on examples and code, this book talks in concepts. The author, Andriy Burkov, walks you through the how and why behind not only the basic concepts, such as what Machine Learning is exactly, but also provides digestible insight into more advanced parts of the industry, such as Unsupervised Learning.

The interesting part of this book is that it's quite short- not 100 pages, but closer to 136 pages. One one hand, critics may say that this is not enough to cover all of Machine Learning, and they're right. The intention, however, isn't to make you an ML expert overnight- instead the author helps you build the foundational knowledge you need to develop a working proficiency in a wide array of Machine Learning topics.

Bonus: Towards Data Science - Medium

While not a book, Medium's content under the "Towards Data Science" banner should be on any aspiring data professional's reading list. For those unaware, Medium is a platform where anyone can post content on almost any topic (but much is focused on work and careers). While the quality and accuracy of the content can be hit-or-miss on Towards Data Science, there are many great pieces by accomplished data professionals. It's definitely worth your time to check out at least the most popular articles and see what you think.

Data Discounts

Because most aspiring data professionals are price conscious regardless of their path, we've pulled together some links to discounts for each of the top three platforms. We're excited to give this to you because we've heard some wonderful stories about how learners have gotten a high-quality education in data for free, or nearly free, by leveraging simple online coupons. Anything we can do to lighten the financial load of breaking into the field of data is a "win" in our book.

A few things to keep in mind:

Look for the best deal you can on the platform you've chosen, not the other way around, ie. don't choose a platform because it has the best discount or even the cheapest cost. If you haven't chosen yet, try going back to "Breakdown of Top 3 Online Platforms" to learn more about which platform meets your needs best.

Don't "wait for a good deal". Promotions can be seasonal, and it's possible that some of these platforms will have slightly better discounts during the holiday season. Don't let a few dollars slow you down on your journey to a career in data. As you know from reading our chapters, there is a lot of effort required to move into a great role, so it's best to get started soon. Remember also that there is a lot of free content on these platforms as elsewhere that can help you hit the ground running.

Here are the discount links. One note- these are not affiliate links, and we make no money when you purchase coursework through one of these platforms.

U UDACITY

Udacity: Can range from 10% to 50% off the cost of verified program (including Nanodegrees)

https://view.everafterguide.net/udacity.com

https://www.couponbirds.com/codes/udacity.com

https://www.sayweee.com/coupons/udacity

coursera

Coursera: Can be a percentage off the price, but is more often either "Free Access" to content or a Free Trial period, sometimes up to a month

https://www.groupon.com/coupons/stores/coursera.org

https://www.retailmenot.com/view/coursera.org

https://www.coupons.com/coupon-codes/coursera/

edX: These coupons are mostly percentages off, and are usually in the 10-20% range. Occasionally you'll find a free trial coupon.

https://www.retailmenot.com/view/edx.org

https://coupons.cnn.com/edx

https://coupons.businessinsider.com/edx

One more tip, you can use browser extensions like Honey or Wikibuy that will automatically search the internet for coupon codes when you're about to purchase from one of these platforms. These work well and are often more comprehensive than searching online yourself.

Honey: https://www.joinhoney.com/

Wikibuy: https://wikibuy.com/

Made in the USA
Columbia, SC
06 April 2020